WOMEN OF KENT RALLY TO THE CAUSE:
A STUDY OF WOMEN'S SUFFRAGE IN EAST KENT
1909 - 1918

Laura Probert

MILLICENT PRESS

WOMEN OF KENT RALLY TO THE CAUSE

Copyright © Laura Probert 2008

All Rights Reserved

No part of this book may be reproduced in any form, by photocopying or by any electronic or mechanical means, Including information storage or retrieval systems, without permission in writing from both the copyright owner and the publisher of this book.

ISBN 978-0-9558674-0-8

This paperback edition first published in 2008 by:
Millicent Press
PO Box 441
Ramsgate
CT11 7WU

Printed in Great Britain for Millicent Press by
Thanet Press Ltd, Union Crescent, Margate, Kent CT9 1NU

WOMEN OF KENT RALLY TO THE CAUSE:
A STUDY OF WOMEN'S SUFFRAGE IN EAST KENT
1909 – 1918

Dedication

To my parents Bill and Freda Willatts, without whom I would never have gone to Guernsey and met Katie Gliddon!

I also owe a great debt to my grandmothers Elizabeth Willatts and Florence Beaumont, who both lived in Kent for at least part of their lives, and whose tales of their youth encouraged my interest in women's lives during the period 1890 – 1918.

"The best part of books is when things are happening. That is the best part of real things too. This is why I shall not tell you in this story about all the days when nothing happened. You will not catch me saying. "Thus the sad days passed slowly by" or "the years rolled on their weary course" or "time went on" – because it is silly; of course time goes on – whether you say so or not. So I shall just tell you the nice interesting parts – and in between you will understand that we had our meals and got up and went to bed, and dull things like that."

Chapter II of the Story of the Treasure Seekers by Edith Nesbit, 1899

Contents

Page

Introduction		1
Chapter One	Women's fight for the cause	5
Chapter Two	South-East Kent in Edwardian times	13
Chapter Three	What Edwardian women wore at the seaside	23
Chapter Four	Early days in the struggle	41
Chapter Five	Anti-suffrage activity in East Kent	45
Chapter Six	1908 – 1909	53
Chapter Seven	1910	67
Chapter Eight	1911 and 1912	81
Chapter Nine	January – June 1913	95
Chapter Ten	July – December 1913	111
Chapter Eleven	January – August 1914	125
Chapter Twelve	Women of Kent on the front line	133
Chapter Thirteen	Women's right to serve	151
Conclusion		157
Appendix		159
Index		161

Introduction

My interest in suffragettes began when I was eight years old. I went to Guernsey with my family that summer and we stayed at a guesthouse in the centre of the island. There was an elderly lady staying there. She had a kind face and her long silver hair was swept up in two loops on each side of her head secured and with a black velvet ribbon. I thought she was very elegant and sophisticated. Her name was Katie Gliddon and she told us she had been a suffragette. I had never heard the word before but loved the sound of it. Miss Gliddon was an artist who specialised in watercolours of flowers. She lived in South Croydon and had studied art at the Slade School in London. In 1910 she was advertising in *Votes for Women* as a teacher of drawing and painting "privately and in schools". My mother and I were invited to an exhibition of her work in central London several months after meeting her in Guernsey. I still have several postcards that Miss Gliddon sent to my mother. Some of her personal papers are now kept at the Women's Library in Whitechapel, but have not yet been catalogued.

Katie Gliddon had hidden a hammer in her muff and on 4th March 1912 had broken a glass panel of a Post Office door in Wimpole Street in Central London. She was arrested and taken to Marylebone Police Station where she was charged with doing wilful damage to the value of £4.10s. Using the pseudonym Katherine Gray she was sentenced to two months hard labour in Holloway Prison. While in prison she asked for a long list of items to be brought in to her including soap, fruit, smelling salts and some old boots!

Most of my research centres around the changing lives of women in the late nineteenth and early twentieth century mainly in the British Isles and Germany. The social history in the years from 1880 until 1920 has always interested me, but especially the Edwardian era. I live in an Edwardian house in Ramsgate, a seaside town in Thanet, an area of East Kent on the south-eastern tip of England, and am preparing a series of illustrated talks about the lives of women in the area. Having just completed a talk on the life of Dame Janet Stancomb-Wills, Ramsgate's first lady mayor and the town's greatest benefactress, I decided to do some research on suffrage activity at a local level.

Most of my research was done in various Kent libraries where I scanned local newspapers from 1909 until 1914, although I also visited the Women's Library in Whitechapel and Manchester Central Library. While in Manchester I went to visit the Pankhurst Centre. This house, once lived in by the Pankhursts after Dr Pankhurst died, was nearly lost in the 1960s but still remains, dwarfed by all the hospital buildings around it, as a defiant symbol of women's struggle. It was an immensely humbling experience to stand in the very room, the back parlour, where Emmeline Pankhurst and her supporters founded the WSPU in 1903, when they realised that the ILP or Independent Labour Party was not going to support their campaign.

I have where possible set the local newspaper items within their national context. I have written in some length about how women coped during the First World War as East Kent was experiencing aerial bombardment for the first time in history and families living on the south-east coast were very much on the front line, living in terror of tip-and-run raids on a daily basis.

Introduction

Illustrations

Most of the history books and biographies which have been written about the suffragettes concentrate mainly on the leaders of the movement such as the Pankhursts, Flora Drummond and Mrs Pethick-Lawrence. Most of the photographs still in existence, such as those by Christina Broom, were taken at the big suffrage events in London. Few papers published any photographs before the First World War although the *Dover Express* was a notable exception.

I had a stroke of luck when Margate Library put a lady in touch with me, Diana Spence, who turned out to be the grand-daughter of one of the suffragists who had been active in Margate in 1913, Beatrice Chapman. She has given me biographical details about her grandmother and allowed me to publish a photograph of her. My most treasured possession, however, has to be Beatrice's NUWSS badge and ribbon, which Diana has kindly given to me!

Suffragettes provided ample subject matter for Edwardian cartoonists in periodicals such as *Punch*, but cartoons were also used to great effect in the suffrage weekly newspapers such as *The Common Cause* or *Votes for Women*. Several women such as Mary Lowndes, Hilda Dallas and the Australian suffragist Dora Meeson Coates became well-known artists in this field, producing many of the most memorable banners and posters, some of which are still reproduced today.

In the absence of photographs I have used mainly fashion advertisements from local ladies' outfitters in Kent at the time, and copied articles from the women's pages relating to the latest fashions. I have also used seaside postcards of the period, to place the suffrage campaign firmly in its social and historical context. Most of the pictures used are from my own collection, any others used are acknowledged in the text.

Editorial note

In local newspapers, *Kelly's Directories* and other publications of the early years of the twentieth century most addresses were written in the hyphenated form, as in "Cecil-square" or "Lyndhurst-avenue". I have decided for clarity to write these addresses, where relevant, as we would write them today.

I give the name in full the first time I mention them but otherwise use the following abbreviations throughout the book:

Organizations

WSPU	Women's Social and Political Union
NUWSS	National Union of Women's Suffrage Societies
WFL	Women's Freedom League
ILP	Independent Labour Party

Newspapers

CC	*The Common Cause*
DE	*Dover Express & East Kent News*
DTEKG	*Dover Times & East Kent Guardian*
EKT	*East Kent Times*

Women in Kent

FH	*Folkestone, Hythe, Sandgate & Cheriton Herald*
IOTG	*Isle of Thanet Gazette*
KGCP	*Kentish Gazette & Canterbury Press*
KMRGEKA	*Keble's Margate & Ramsgate Gazette & East Kent Advertiser*
TT	*Thanet Times*
VW	*Votes for Women*

Acknowledgements and thanks

All the following people and organizations have encouraged me to persevere and have helped me with my research – David Doughan and staff at the Women's Library, Ros Arnold and Anna Kitchen at the Pankhurst Centre in Manchester, Diana Spence, Jennifer Smith, Anne Ward, Marie Selwood, Peggy White, Anne Logan, Tony Rees, Helena Wojtczak, Ralph Hoult, Manchester Central Library, Margate Museum and Margate Library, Folkestone Local Studies Library, Canterbury Local Studies Library and Dover Discovery Centre.

Richard Clements, a local Thanet collector of postcards and seaside memorabilia, kindly gave me permission to use one of his postcards to illustrate this book. His book of *Margate in Old Photographs* in the Sutton Publishing series, provides a fascinating glimpse into life in an Edwardian seaside resort.

Laura Probert
Ramsgate 2007

Biographical

Laura is a semi-retired librarian living in Ramsgate in Kent. She cares passionately about the town she lives in and through her illustrated talks and a series of books intends to raise the profile of women's history in East Kent. Her other interests include steam trains, Roman archaeology and life in the Edwardian era.

Chapter One

Women's fight for the cause

A permanent and vast difference of type has been impressed upon women and men respectively by the Maker of both. Their differences of social office rest mainly upon causes, not flexible and elastic like most mental qualities, but physical and in their nature unchangeable. I for one am not prepared to say which of the two sexes has the higher and which has the lower province. But I recognize the subtle and profound character of the differences between them. (William Ewart Gladstone in a letter to Samuel Smith MP, 11th April 1892)

Why were women forced to fight for the right to vote?

Following the publication of Mary Wollstonecraft's *Vindication of the Rights of Women* in 1792, the issue of women's suffrage first arose in the British Parliament when Charles Grey proposed a motion for parliamentary reform in 1797. Mary had written: "I do not wish them to have power over men; but over themselves." Charles James Fox suggested that better-educated women deserved the franchise more than the least-educated and more dependent classes of men, such as soldiers and servants. Fox was trying to show up the inconsistencies in positions in the demands of those asking for expansion of male suffrage rather than making a serious proposal for the enfranchisement of women.

Mrs Snowden summed it up very neatly during her visit to Margate in February 1909.

> Until 1832 there was no law in existence that prevented women from voting. Not many did but it should be borne in mind that at the time the total electorate numbered only 600,000. There was a very high property qualification which very few women could maintain. In 1832 women lost the franchise when men substituted the word 'man' for the word 'person' in the law books.[1]

> *Mrs Ethel Snowden was the wife of Philip Snowden MP who had been elected as ILP candidate in Blackburn in 1906. They both came from Yorkshire and met at a Fabian Society meeting in Leeds. Mrs Snowden persuaded her husband to support women's suffrage and she became one of the main speakers of the NUWSS. She had been on a speaking tour of the United States in 1908, and in 1909 accompanied Mrs Pankhurst to Canada to address the Canadian Suffrage Association in Ontario.*

In August 1832 Henry Hunt, MP for Preston, presented a petition from Mary Smith in Yorkshire who claimed that, as she paid taxes, she had a right to vote. Mr Hunt had been in prison following his attempt to speak to 80,000 people, at St Peter's Fields in Manchester in August 1819, about male parliamentary reform. Local magistrates ordered the cavalry to break up the meeting and in the ensuing chaos eleven people were killed. These events became known as the Peterloo Massacre.

A clause in the first draft of the People's Charter, published in May 1838, called for universal suffrage. William Lovett wanted to include the enfranchisement of women with universal male suffrage but his friends dissuaded him as they thought the suggestion would not be taken seriously.

In 1865 a group of women who were hoping to pursue careers in medicine or the other professions formed a discussion group in London called the Kensington Society. The group included Barbara Bodichon, Emily Davies, Helen Taylor and Elizabeth Garrett. They discussed parliamentary reform and drafted a petition asking Parliament to grant women the vote. Helen Taylor was the stepdaughter of John Stuart Mill, MP for Westminster, so they asked him and Henry Fawcett MP to present their petition to the House of Commons. The petition asked for suitably qualified women to be included in the Second Reform Bill on the grounds that taxation and representation could not be separated. On 7th June 1866 Elizabeth Garrett walked into the Palace of Westminster carrying a large roll of parchment containing 1,500 signatures.

The women's demand was outvoted by 194 to 73 but working-class men in towns did gain the right to vote. John Stuart Mill had worked with Dr Richard Marsden Pankhurst to draft an amendment to re-enfranchise women on the same terms as men. One of the largest collections of signatures ever made was sent to Parliament but the amendment was killed in debate. The women were very disappointed and decided then to form the London Society for Women's Suffrage.

In the 1860s and 1870s, Millicent Fawcett in London, Flora Stevenson in Edinburgh and Lydia Becker in Manchester worked hard promoting their cause, speaking in large towns and cities throughout the British Isles. Seventeen local groups joined together to form the NUWSS. Lydia Becker was editor of the *Women's Suffrage Journal* throughout the 1870s and 1880s. In 1887 she was elected as president of the NUWSS but unfortunately died three years later.

In 1869 John Stuart Mill published his work on *The Subjection of Women* and in Chapter III we find the following statement: "Under whatever conditions, and within whatever limits, men are admitted to the suffrage, there is not a shadow of justification for not admitting women under the same."

That same year, women who owned property gained the right to vote in local elections, but not in General Elections, despite being taxpayers. It was also in 1869 that Dr Richard Pankhurst had been responsible for the municipal vote being restored to women. He also campaigned for the Married Women's Property Act, which when passed in 1882 allowed a wife to retain for herself her inheritance and earnings.

The new woman leads the way

In the 1880s term "new woman" was coined to describe women of the new educated generation who were more assertive and self-confident. They wanted the chance to train in the professions on the same terms as men, and were independent thinkers who met to debate many of the topical issues.

Women's fight for the cause

During the Edwardian period women were achieving great things throughout Europe and in the United States. Women such as Marie Stopes, Octavia Hill, Emma Cons, Marie Curie (the Nobel Prize-winning scientist), Rosa Luxemburg, Klara Zetkin, Beatrice Webb, Elizabeth Garrett Anderson and Edith Nesbit, to name but a few, were campaigning, inventing, discovering and creating. By 1910 women such as Raymonde de la Roche and Meli Beese were quite literally taking to the skies.

Middle-class women were asking to be treated on equal terms with men on matters such as property, wages and divorce rights. They also demanded equal access to education and careers. These women no longer accepted that women's horizons should be restricted to marriage, childbirth, housework and low-paid wage labour. They were indignant that society undervalued them and that women's talents and potential were being wasted.

In 1884 the right to vote was extended to working-class men in rural areas but women were still excluded, even though they had by now won the right to work as nurses, teachers and factory workers.

In 1893 the women in New Zealand, including the Maori women, became the first to be granted the vote on 19th September 1893. There is a memorial in Christchurch to commemorate this very important event (*above*).

In 1895 the British General Election returned a number of MPs sympathetic to women's suffrage. Encouraged by this support the women's suffrage campaign gained momentum and thousands of women all over the country rallied to "the Cause", as it became known.

In 1897 the National Union of Women's Suffrage Societies, or NUWSS, became an official organisation with Millicent Fawcett as President. The suffrage campaign in Britain became focussed, and later the tactics of the more militant suffragists ensured that their crusade received maximum publicity.

In 1902 a delegation of women textile workers from Northern England presented a petition to Parliament containing 37,000 signatures demanding "Votes for Women".

In October 1903 Mrs Emmeline Pankhurst founded the Women's Social and Political Union in Manchester to give a political voice to the women who wanted to vote and participate as equals with men in the newly formed Independent Labour Party.

On 12th May 1905 the Women's Suffrage Bill introduced by Bamford Slack MP was talked out in the House of Commons accompanied by much laughter and coarse jokes. On 19th May 1905 a group of ten women, including 76-year-old Emily Davies, went to hand in the women's suffrage petition to the Prime Minister. He asked them to be patient!

Suffragists were disappointed and proposed a more militant campaign.

Women of Kent
Deeds not words!

In October 1905 Christabel Pankhurst and Annie Kenney were the first women to be arrested in the fight for female suffrage when they assaulted police at a Liberal Party meeting in Manchester. They opted for a seven-day prison sentence instead of paying the fine.

The term **suffragette** was first used by the *Daily Mail* in January 1906 as a derogatory term to describe the more militant women in the WSPU. It was also in 1906 that Finland became the first European country to give women the vote.

In May 1906 a delegation of women from both the WSPU and the NUWSS met with the Prime Minister, Sir Henry Campbell Bannerman. The group included Emmeline Pankhurst, Annie Kenney, Mrs Wolstenholme-Elmy and Emmeline Pethick-Lawrence. Keir Hardie also joined them. The Prime Minister was not very encouraging. Annie Kenney stood up and shouted "Sir, we are not satisfied! The agitation will go on."

Millicent Garrett Fawcett, founder member of the NUWSS in 1897, organised their first national demonstration in London on 11th February 1907 . It became known as "The Mud March" because of the terrible weather at the time. Forty societies were represented in the procession which also included carriages and motor cars. Two meetings were held afterwards in Trafalgar Square and the Exeter Hall, where the speakers included Miss Eva Gore-Booth, one time secretary of Manchester Women's Trade Council, who later became the first woman to be elected to the British Parliament under her married name of Countess Markievicz.

In March 1907 this article discussing the desirability of giving women votes for parliamentary elections, which was reprinted from *The Globe,* appeared in *Keble's Margate & Ramsgate Gazette &East Kent Advertiser*:

Votes for Women

Discussing the desirability of giving women votes for Parliamentary elections, the *Globe* says:- The truth is that this matter has not yet been properly thought out, and that a great deal of much more thorough discussion than has yet been expended upon it must be gone through before Parliament can safely express a decided opinion one way or the other. That there are thousands of women in the country who by their intelligence and by the large interests which they control are a great deal better qualified to exercise an influence upon the policy of the country than the male supporters of the Wastrels and the Socialists, no sensible person would deny. But one of the first elements of the problem is to discover whether these women want the vote or prefer to exercise their legitimate influences upon policy by more indirect but certainly, not less powerful means. The answer to that question is, to say the least of it, exceedingly doubtful, and until Parliament is satisfied that the vote is really desired by the majority of the women in the country, it would be wrong to take any steps towards giving it. Woman's physical nature is wholly different from that of man, and it is a more common-place to say that she has not his fitness for the rough and tumble of the outside world. Is she to decide on wars in which she will never be called upon to fight, or is it not rather her place to exercise from the sanctity of home an influence which will restrain the impetuous from rash quarrels, or spur on the timid to obey the call of honour? To her is committed the sacred right to be the mother of the men that are to be, and to inspire them with a sense of their

Women's fight for the cause

destiny as the sons of an Imperial race. We gravely question whether that exquisite duty is compatible with a share in the sordid game of politics, and we are certain that it would be an incalculable loss to the nation to acquire a new class of voter at the sacrifice of the realities of Wifehood and Motherhood, and all that they mean."[2]

In October 1907 Emmeline Pethick-Lawrence and her husband Frederick launched the suffragette newspaper *Votes for Women*. That same month the Women's Freedom League was formed when Teresa Billington-Grieg, Charlotte Despard and others, no longer able to tolerate the leadership and tactics of the Pankhursts, broke away from the WSPU.

Margate Beach ca 1910

The Qualification of Women Act of 1907 allowed for the first time the election of women onto borough and county councils, and their election as mayor. This was an important step as, though women had been attending meetings, they had not been allowed to vote. Emma Cons, the founder of the Old Vic Theatre and Morley College in Lambeth, was an active suffragist. She had been elected as the first woman Alderman of the newly formed LCC or London County Council in 1889.

Two women were elected to the council in 1889 – Lady Margaret Sandhurst (Brixton) and Miss Jane Cobden (Bow). A third, Miss Cons, was selected as an alderman. The women members' right to sit on the LCC was immediately challenged by the extreme anti-suffragist Mr Beresford-Hope who had been defeated by Lady Sandhurst. Lady Sandhurst took her case to the House of Lords in which it was decided that women are incapacitated from being elected members of a county council. The case was an important one relating to the franchise question for women.

Women of Kent

Lord Esher, one of the judges, and Master of the Rolls said: "I take it that by neither the common law nor the constitution of this country from the beginning of the common law until now (1889) can a woman be entitled to exercise any public function."

The judges in this case had to interpret the Municipal Corporations Act, in which the word "person" is used throughout. It was held that the right to be elected was NOT conferred by the Act, but only the right to vote, the word "person" not being regarded by the judges as including women!

A woman, for the purposes of citizenship, had no legal existence in England, and had to be created before she could be enfranchised! A woman could be a criminal, a queen, a tax and rate-payer and owner of property, but she could not be a citizen of Great Britain and Ireland until a right to become such had been created by an Act of Parliament.

In 1889 Emma Cons attended 69 out of a possible 89 committee meetings where she spoke up for women asylum patients, sanitation, and theatres and music halls, but she was not allowed to vote on these issues. She resigned when the other female councillors were unseated.

The pioneering doctor, Elizabeth Garrett Anderson became in 1908 the first woman to be elected as a mayor in Aldeburgh in Suffolk. Dame Janet Stancomb-Wills, who came to live in Ramsgate in 1911, was the first woman to be elected on to a borough council, in Kent in 1913. In 1923 she became the first woman mayor of Ramsgate.

After Lloyd George's announcement on 27th January 1913 that the reform Bill was withdrawn, Mrs Pankhurst launched a campaign of "guerrilla militancy". She claimed that the suffragettes were not going to injure human beings, but, if the campaign was to have an impact on the fight to win the vote, "they were going to do as much damage to their property as they possibly could".

The back of the NUWSS membership card for the Dover branch in 1911 reads as follows:

Why Women should have the Vote

Because legislators never have troubled themselves, and never will till women are voters, as to how a proposed law may adversely affect women.

As proof of this no woman is the legal parent of her own child unless it is illegitimate, our divorce laws are unequal and grossly unfair to women, whilst the law gives the right to a man to take away from his wife every penny that may have been saved by their united efforts. Further the law as to intestacy and on other points is full of numerous injustices to women.

The testimony of Statesmen in countries where women do vote is that it has proved of vast benefit to the country.

The Annual Subscription to the Society is One Shilling.

You will greatly help the cause if you join the Society, even if you do not wish to take an active part in the work.

By 1914 the campaign for *Votes for Women* had become increasingly bitter with women being imprisoned and force-fed. Militant suffragettes continued their arson and sabotage attacks on railway stations, piers, sports pavilions etc. One-hundred

Women's fight for the cause

and-forty-one acts of destruction were chronicled in the press during the first seven months of 1914.

Even at its peak in 1914 the WSPU only had about 2,000 members. The non-militant NUWSS was a much larger organization. The number of branches rose from 33 in October 1907 to almost 500 local branches in 1914. The 22,000 membership in January 1911 had more than doubled by February 1914.

---

[1] TT 17th February 1909
[2] KMRGEKA 16th February 1907

Chapter Two

South-East Kent in Edwardian Times

No one can tell what it is in the Air of Margate, but practical experience has proved that none better can be found. (Sir James Paget, Bart. FRS, FRCS quoted in *Thanet Times* 7th July 1909)

Thanet

The Isle of Thanet in East Kent comprises of several seaside towns and villages. On the north Kent coast there are Margate and Cliftonville with Birchington and Westgate. Facing south-east are Broadstairs and Ramsgate and the village of Pegwell Bay.

According to the Ramsgate *Kelly's Street Directory* of 1914–1915, Ramsgate was:

> ... a town of importance celebrated both as a watering-place and a place of commerce; and it is distinguished for its fine harbour, so useful to the mariner as well as attractive to the public for the promenade along the pier. Its sands have a high reputation as a bathing station and are famed as a lounge – the scene on which in the season has been so graphically portrayed by the great painter, Mr Frith.

This is a reference to the famous painting entitled *Ramsgate Sands* painted in 1854, and now in the Queen's collection. Many of the buildings shown in this painting are easily recognisable today. The photograph (above) shows Thanet people posing on Ramsgate Sands in 2004 for a 150-year anniversary reconstruction of the original Frith painting. The author is next to the young soldier on the right!

In May 1912 the Ramsgate Advertising Committee reported that it had supplied the South Eastern and Chatham Railway with 500 coloured views of

Ramsgate for exhibition in railway carriages. A further supply of 10,000 guides and 10,000 pictorial posters had been ordered, as they were well aware that "such towns as Ramsgate, in order to compete with other holiday resorts, which are advertising very extensively, must adopt the same methods".

The Committee was also anxious to thank all the railway companies who were advertising the improved through-railway services to Ramsgate.[1] The Granville Hotel on Ramsgate's East Cliff, seen in this old postcard, used to advertise itself as "the leading hotel in Ramsgate" which the advertisement claimed was "the most bracing and invigorating seaside resort in England".

The Margate *Kelly's Street Directory* for 1900 states that "the salubrity of Margate air is proverbial. And the excellence and safety of its sea-bathing is certainly one of its chief attractions. The large expanse of sands, which are dry and hard at low tide, afford a capital playground for the host of children annually brought down by their parents." The good air was also beneficial to sick people

from the overcrowded insanitary metropolis. The Royal Sea Bathing Hospital had opened in Margate in the 1790s and specialized in treating tubercular diseases. Benjamin Beale's bathing machines had first appeared on Margate beaches as early as 1750.

South-East Kent in Edwardian Times

In 1905 Margate and Cliftonville were marketed as separate resorts. "Merry Margate! Healthy Margate!" was "catering for the million, with its Jetty, its sands, and general air of jollity and freedom from restraint". Cliftonville was more select and with "its charming promenades, its beautiful sands and sea-bathing, its shady park" was a district "as quiet and select as the most fastidious could desire".[2]

The original Ramsgate Town Station

Thanet a hundred years ago was very different from now. The London, Chatham and Dover Railway had linked the island with the metropolis in 1863. Only two hours from London by train all the separate towns on the island were popular with wealthier families, who often moved their whole households down to the south coast during the summer months, bringing their servants with them. The old Ramsgate Town Station was opposite the top of Chatham Street.

Fathers would come down for the weekend then return to the City by an early train on Monday morning. Other trippers arrived by paddle steamers from Tower Bridge, embarking at the ends of fragile iron piers ready to enjoy the delights of Italian ice cream and fish and chip suppers. Many local families let rooms to summer boarders for "five meals and a bed at two guineas per week".

The husbands quite enjoyed their steamer trips down to Kent. On Friday afternoons "Husbands – young husbands, middle-aged husbands, old husbands, rich husbands, poor husbands, in fact, every kind of husband" boarded the steamer at Tower Bridge. "Camp-stools and deck-chairs are placed in the selected spots, the order given to cast off, and we are away, gliding on our road to meet our loved ones, the flat Essex shore on our left hand, whilst the sun lights up the beautiful Kentish hills on our right."

The highlight of the trip was the splendid tea available on board:

A Palace steamer tea is a thing to remember. The sharp bracing air has just put the finishing touch to our appetites, and it is with a smile of approbation that we glance at the well-laid tables. Lobsters in their shining red coats, huge Scotch salmon, barons of beef, chickens, ham, tongues, while fruit and salads, cakes and sweets galore complete the menu.

Women in Kent

After tea the men strolled on deck "with lighted pipes and caps pressed firmly on our foreheads – at peace with all the world ".[3]

Day-trippers were not so popular with guest house and restaurant owners as they discouraged the more well-to-do guests. They did not spend much money as they usually brought their own food in picnic baskets with them and ate it on the beach.

A seasonal army of entertainers, photographers, pickpockets and other get-rich-quick entrepreneurs descended on the seaside like a plague of locusts ready to exploit the summer visitors. There were sandcastle competitions, Punch and Judy shows, donkey rides (also known as Jerusalem ponies) and goat carts.

Visits from an occasional seaplane or aeroplane also provided popular viewing especially if advertised in the local newspaper in advance! Of course pilots were not very experienced so accidents were increasingly common, and, as can be seen here at Boughton Hill near Canterbury, their mishaps also drew inquisitive crowds.

South-East Kent in Edwardian Times

Following Louis Bleriot's successful attempt to fly across the Channel in July 1909 it was agreed early in 1910 to erect a monument on the cliff top near Dover Castle where he had landed. The concrete monument is still there today. On 2nd June 1910 Charles Rolls, one half of the Rolls–Royce partnership, became the first Englishman to cross the Channel by plane. Towards the end of July a Frenchwoman, Madame Franck, was hoping to attempt the crossing in her Farman bi-plane, but unfortunately a few days beforehand she crashed near Durham and broke her left leg in two places. "A lad was struck by the engine and instantly killed. The Coroner remarked that the crowd's great interest in the novelty of flying led them to disregard discretion."[4] In the *Isle of Thanet Gazette*, 27th April 1912, we read that: "Aeroplanes are becoming quite as common at Margate as taxi-cabs or motor char-a-bancs, and all people are suffering from what has been not inappropriately dubbed 'Aeroplanitis',"

The women's section of Pettman's bathing station at Walpole Bay

There was always plenty to watch on the water too, with steamers arriving from London, Thames barges, fishing boats and the occasional launching of the lifeboat. The more adventurous took a dip in the sea. In 1906 Pettman's Sea Bathing platform between Newgate Gap and Walpole Bay offered one of the first mixed bathing opportunities in England. Visitors hired bathing dresses which covered them from the neck to the knees.[5] The Pettman name can still be seen on the old depository building in Athelstan Road.

Dan Leno, the music hall entertainer, sang about a swimming master:

> On the pier in the summer-time there am I
> Teaching the ladies to swim
> Though frightened at first of the water they be
> Their confidence soon will return, don't you see
> When they have feasted their eyes upon me
> And noticed my figure so trim.

Women in Kent

If you were fed up with sitting on the beach there were different excursions around the island in horse-drawn brakes or carriages. Or you could travel on the Isle of Thanet Electric Tramway which was opened in 1901. By 1914 horse-drawn vehicles were being replaced by long open-topped motorized charabancs. Favourite destinations included Pegwell Bay (famous for its shrimps), Richborough Castle, The Brown Jug at Dumpton, Grove Ferry, and the village of Minster.

"A casual visitor" writing in the *Dover Express* also described the delights of the "hills and vales of East Kent" such as the Alkham Valley, Elham Valley and Wye Valley, and asks "how many of the English people who annually tramp over to Europe know of the loveliness of these Kentish hills and dales?" They also mention the ancient Roman Road linking Studfall Castle at Lympne with Canterbury but bemoan the fact that "it now needs widening in places to allow two vehicles comfortably to pass, and to make it less perilous for pedestrians when the motor cars rush by as though they were racing and out-distancing an Elham Valley train."[6]

Dover, Folkestone and Canterbury were also popular destinations. Dover and Folkestone were thriving as seaside resorts but were also the main ports for packet boats to travel to the Continent. Canterbury, with its beautiful Cathedral, was still a quaint market town which had been playing host to visitors ever since Thomas à Becket was murdered in 1170. Deal, a Cinque port with its pier and its Tudor Rose castle was another town popular with summer visitors. If the weather was poor the families could go into one of the numerous dining-rooms, or go shopping for souvenirs and postcards. This picture (*left*) shows Harbour Street in Ramsgate in about 1910 crowded with shoppers. Crested china was a popular purchase, or perhaps they went to a studio to pose for a family photograph. On fine days photographs were taken on the beach, or sometimes in groups outside their hotel or lodging-house. These could be sent to relatives as a postcard later the same day.

Entertainment

Minstrels, pierrots and other entertainers performed on the beach three times daily during the summer. All the Thanet resorts had tea-gardens, bandstands and at least one theatre. The Winter Gardens built into the cliff in Margate opened in 1911. The Royal Victoria Pavilion in Ramsgate opened in 1903. In 1905 they were offering a weekly change of programme in Grand Variety Entertainment and Biograph and at the weekends: "The Band Plays on Saturday Afternoons from 3.00 to 4.30 on the Promenade (if wet inside the Theatre). Admission 2d" and "A Grand Concert Every Sunday Evening at 8 pm. Admission 6d, 1/-, 1/6". They were also offering "a series of Dances (with lime-light effects) in the Grand Hall during the summer and winter months. Admission 1/-".[7]

Many of the popular music hall stars and actors such as Vesta Tilley, Marie Lloyd and Ellen Terry came to Thanet during the summer.

In August 1907 Miss Ellen Terry (*above right*) played to packed houses for three nights at the Theatre Royal in Margate in George Bernard Shaw's play *Captain Brassbound's Conversion*. The audience was curious to see her new husband, the American actor James Carew "who recently married Miss Terry under such romantic circumstances". Shaw had written the play in 1901 and persuaded Ellen Terry to act the part of Lady Cicely Waynflete. Her husband played Captain Brassbound. Sadly the marriage only lasted two years as James was many years younger than his new wife. Ellen Terry was a keen suffragist. She took part in the Pageant of Great Women in 1909 with her daughter, costume designer Edith Craig.

Towards the end of August 1914 over 2000 people packed Margate's Winter Gardens to see one of England's favourite music hall stars, the male-impersonator, Miss Vesta Tilley (*right*). It was her first visit to Margate and she "had an almost royal welcome and bouquets and other gifts were showered upon her, and when she left the building in her private automobile at the close the enthusiasm was unbounded". One of the most popular numbers that night was "The man who broke the bank at Monte Carlo". She ended her magnificent performance with a patriotic song fitting for the occasion. Afterwards she graciously acknowledged the extraordinary warmth of her reception with an eloquent speech.

Women in Kent

Vesta Tilley and her husband ran a military recruitment drive, as did a number of other music-hall stars. In the guise of characters like "Tommy in the Trench" and "Jack Tar Home from Sea", Tilley performed songs such as "The army of today's all right" and "Jolly good luck to the girl who loves a soldier", written for her by her husband which earned her the nickname "Britain's best recruiting sergeant" – young men were sometimes asked to join the army on stage during her show. Vesta Tilley also performed in hospitals and sold War Bonds.

Vesta Tilley retired from the stage in 1920 when her husband Walter de Freece became an MP. He was also part-owner of the Hippodrome Music Hall in Margate and was knighted in 1919 for his services to the war effort. Wounded soldiers were invited to matinee performances at the Hippodrome free of charge. Regular Sunday afternoon services for the soldiers were held in the winter throughout the war. This advertisement for Marie Lloyd dates from slightly earlier, August 1908. The Hippodrome was on the site of the present Margate Library and Thanet District Council Offices facing Cecil Square. Of interest are the different prices ranging from 15/- (fifteen shillings) for a private box to 3d (threepence) in the gallery or gods. Marie Lloyd was one of the most popular musical hall artistes of her day and she was the champion of the working classes. Her best-known numbers included "My old man said follow the van", "O Mr Porter", and "The boy I love is up in the gallery".

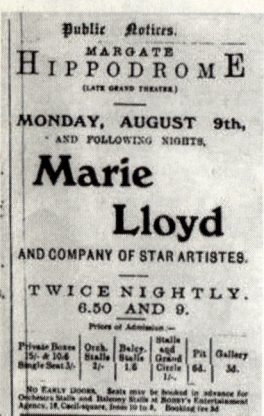

An ideal campaigning ground

In August 1910 a well-dressed lady called Lavendar Baillie-Guthrie appeared in the dock before the Margate Borough Justices to answer a summons under the Borough Bye Laws for chalking on the footpath along the Fort Green Promenade on July 10th. The defendant admitted that she was a member of the WSPU and that she had chalked "Votes for women" on the public promenade, but asked why all the other persons who had chalked notices about lost articles etc had not been summoned as well. The defendant when questioned stated that she was a visitor to Margate and would be leaving that afternoon. She agreed to abide by the bye law and the case was dismissed.[8]

This article is interesting because it highlights the fact that the suffragists came to the Kentish seaside towns in large numbers during the summer months. Women were freer at the seaside than they normally were at home. Often they were alone from Monday to Friday without their husbands so could attend political meetings or spend more time associating with other women.

Only two hours from London by train Thanet was an ideal campaigning ground as there were numerous halls and entertainment venues which could be hired for meetings. In fine weather, meetings could be held on the beaches. From Monday to Friday the population of these resorts was largely female as the husbands went back to work in the metropolis during the week. The influx of

South-East Kent in Edwardian Times

holiday visitors and summer boarders was a captive audience, and the suffragist newspapers ran an active campaign to encourage their members to sell papers and recruit new members in the seaside towns.

The Common Cause reminded readers of their "Holiday task" and added "The Editor is going for a holiday – the first for three years. She would like to come back to a doubled circulation!"[9]

> Suffragist visitors to the Kentish coast are responding splendidly to the organiser's appeal for help. Miss Elsie Douglas, who is staying at Hythe, has volunteered to help in Folkestone while Miss V H Friedlaender, with her mother and brother, is undertaking preliminary arrangements for a course of open-air meetings in Deal. Miss Gertrude Harraden has kindly promised to be local Secretary for Walmer, and Miss Mabel Spink to help in Dover, where Mrs Robinson of Sittingbourne will support her.
>
> An open-air campaign is being planned which will extend from Herne Bay round the coast to Folkestone. Visitors willing to help, especially speakers, are urgently asked to communicate at once with the organiser at 2 York Terrace in Ramsgate."[10]

That week's meetings were planned for:

Friday 5th August	Hodgman's Yard, King Street, Ramsgate
Saturday 6th August	The Fountain, Folkestone
Monday 8th August	The beach in Deal
Tuesday 9th August	Rose Inn Yard, Albion Street, Broadstairs
Wednesday 10th August	Cecil Square, Margate

According to the 1914 Ramsgate Street Directory, *Hodgman's Yard in Ramsgate, which Mr Hodgman kindly allowed the women to use as a meeting place, was behind No 30 King Street midway between Broad Street and Brunswick Street.*

The seaside towns of Thanet remained popular resorts for families right up until the 1960s when package holidays by air to warmer and more exotic locations began to tempt holidaymakers away from Britain's south coast resorts.

---

[1] *Thanet Times* 10th May 1912
[2] *Thanet Times* 21st April 1905
[3] *Thanet Times* 11th August 1905
[4] DE 5th August 1910
[5] TT 15th August 1913
[6] DE 5th August 1910
[7] *Ramsgate and Broadstairs by Camera and Pen*, 1904–5, p8
[8] TT 9th August 1910
[9] CC 11th August 1910
[10] VW 5th August 1910

Chapter Three

What Edwardian women wore at the seaside

Silk Frock in Paillette. The Blouse, with a collar embroidered in Broderie Anglaise, made with a fancy shaped effect coming square in front. The bodice and skirt have sets of tucks and are finished with small bead buttons and worked loops. 39/11. (A dress advertised by Lewis, Hyland and Linom in April 1913)

Womens' fashions in the Edwardian era were so feminine and elegant. With their slim waists and swinging ankle-length skirts, topped by often outrageously large hats, the young ladies certainly made heads turn as they walked in twos and threes along the promenade.

Women in Cliftonville in 1909

In the 1890s women had started to wear suits because it was felt that this made them look efficient and capable of doing the same jobs as men. Male caricaturists portrayed women in suits as shapeless ugly women in spectacles and this image was often used to depict suffragettes, so suffrage leaders urged their members to wear their best clothes on the summer marches through London. The surviving images of women marching in suffrage processions immaculately turned out in crisp white summer dresses and trimmed boaters are very powerful, and leave the observer in no doubt about their femininity. It is images like these that most people now associate with the suffrage movement, not the shrieking harridans in the *Punch* cartoons.

Dress decorations

> All kinds of materials are used nowadays for making flowers. There are velvet ones, with the petals painted by hand to show the natural shadings of the blossoms, and there are others exquisitely fashioned by means of delicately and precisely pleated tulle.
>
> How it is manipulated the inexperienced observer is unable to determine, but each crisp petal is perfect, and the result as a whole is absolutely lovely, albeit, of course, of a very artificial aspect.
>
> Dotted muslin makes beautiful flowers. The graceful anemone is a favourite choice in the fashionable purple shade, and that peculiarly delicate grey–blue which looks as if all the colour had been washed out of it, is very becoming.
>
> Glorious golden irises, and purple ones too, are fashioned out of the spot-flecked fabric, and the rose is, of course, a resource of great delight.
>
> It is a pretty notion to trim frocks with pin-spotted muslin flowers, using them in print sprigs or more natural-looking bunches.
>
> A negligee made of white muslin-draped satin has the fichu draperies caught at the left of the waist-line beneath a bunch of roses, one pink, another frost-nipped damask, and a third a bright yet soft amber. The leaves are made of wired muslin and instead of being green, show the brown and russet tints.[1]

These "Fashion Jottings" in *Votes for Women* in November 1911 hint that the "new women" were no longer slaves to fashion but sought more practical solutions when dressing for their rapidly changing lives.

> Is woman becoming emancipated even in the *ateliers* of la Mode? Well I will not comment that most gratuitous of all crimes – prophecy – but it looks like it. Did not our dress autocrats – the inviolate male Cabinet Council of Paris – command not only that straight skirts should be totally tabooed, but, still more terrible, that we were to encumber ourselves with the crinoline? And yet here we are practically as we were. Sleeves are somewhat wider at the elbow. Gowns, except for walking, are longer, and their draperies are more pronounced, But the straight skirt (*bien entendu* not the hideous "hobble") still lives to give us lightness, cleanliness, freedom, and thrice welcome packing-spaces, even in our motor-boxes. Nevertheless, there is no lack of novelty, especially in the new colour effects. Textures, too, are more various and beautiful than ever.[2]

The poem opposite from the New York Times was reprinted in the *Thanet Gazette* in June 1913. This advertisement from the *Thanet Times* in 1905 gives us a wonderful glimpse into the fashion requirements of the day:

> All ladies who intend going to Ramsgate during the coming week should make a point of visiting the large establishment of Springford's, 49 and 51, High-street. The windows of this well-known firm just now are most effectively dressed with every conceivable kind of seasonable novelty appealing to the tastes of the fair sex; and the housewife who cannot satisfy her own particular requirements here would, indeed, be very hard to please.

What Edwardian women wore

One of my ancestors on my mother's side of the family in about 1870

What Grandmother wore

They are saying mean things to our faces
Of the trim little hats that we wear
The close-fitting toques and the turbans
That keep all the dust from the hair
But do they remember the bonnets,
The coal-scuttle bonnets of yore
All loaded with feathers and flowers
The bonnets our grandmothers wore?

The funny cartoonists are flaying
The short, narrow skirt of today
Escaping the germs on the pavement
In wait to be carried away.
Just think of the flounces and scallops
The gathers behind and before
The yards that went sweeping the gutters
In the dresses our grandmothers wore

Their delicate shoulders uncovered
And boards in the front of their stays
Were some of the tortures that custom
Decreed in our grandmothers' days
A waist that was squeezed like a lemon
Pantalets coming down to the floor
And hoops, were a few of the fashions
Our foolish young grandmothers wore

Do you doubt that the world is progressing?
And scoff at out latter-day clothes?
Then go up to the trunks in the garret
Where garments discarded repose
Put on all the finery faded
The petticoats too, by the score
And walk – if you can – in the bundles
Of dry goods our grandmothers wore.[3]

Women in Kent

They were offering "a wonderful collection of high-class millinery, stylish hats, lovely chiffons, delicate laces, aprons, underclothing, dress skirts of latest designs, perfect fitting corsets of all kinds" and assure readers that "The quality of the articles is of the best, while the prices are of the lowest."[4]

In Edwardian England most women wore their hair long so advertisements for hair tonic like the one above often appeared in the local press. On top of their tresses the wealthier Edwardian ladies wore very elegant hats, some of which reached amazing proportions as this amusing article conveys:

> **Huge Hats in Church**
>
> It has generally been understood that ladies' hats of a large and obstructive character have prevented men from attending matinees. But a new cry has arisen! It seems that they interfere with devotion. The church hat is now so large that women devotees in the back pews cannot see the preacher. This complaint comes from newer and perhaps more fashionable churches, where it is customary to raise the pulpit but a few steps from the floor. This may bring the preacher down to the level of his hearers, but it prevents many of the hearers from seeing the preacher because of the big hats of the devout women.[5]

The hat from 1913 in the above drawing might have been the sort of hat they were complaining about. Feathers were a popular trimming especially ostrich plumes, but flowers, either individually or in clusters, were also common, surrounded by generous amounts of ribbon and lace. Some hats had a net veil that could be pulled down over the face. These were not just worn at funerals but early motorists welcomed them too.

What Edwardian women wore

Even poorer working-class women would not usually be seen out in the street without a scarf of shawl covering their head. Some even wore men's caps. These London women who went hop-picking in Kent (*right*) dressed themselves and their children in their best hats to pose for a photograph which was still for them a rare event. If they needed a new hat for a special occasion they just bought some new ribbon or trimmings, or some artificial flowers, and added them to the old hat.

These workers in a shoe factory look as if they have worn their best clothes to work that day because they have been told they will be photographed. They are obviously posing and looking at the camera, and not actually working, as their smart blouses and tidy hair suggest. The woman wearing a blouse and tie is probably a supervisor.

Workers in a shoe factory in 1909

Edwardian women did a lot of walking. Laced boots or walking shoes with a small heel were usually worn. Most working-class women wore boots. Women working in factories often wore clogs to work.

Women all learnt to sew by hand and could make some of their undergarments and blouses. By the early twentieth century many households had treadle sewing-machines so women could make their own outer garments, as well as supplementing their income by repairing clothes or doing fine needlework. Seamstresses and milliners were in great demand, as were laundresses who not only had to wash and starch the clothes, but also had the unenviable task of ironing and pressing all the linen.

Women in Kent

Images of women were being used more often in advertisements, such as this one for the "Rinso Girl" from 1911. Another, advertising a different kind of soap in March 1911, suggests that the woman wearing this very fine wedding gown should "make the most of her charms".

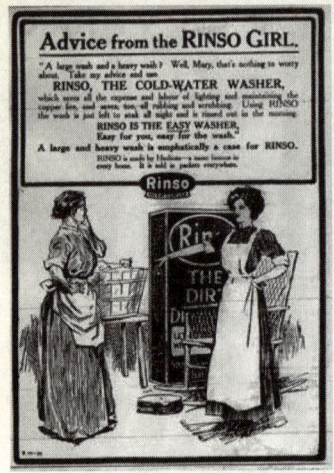 

Many advertisements also hinted that life for women was not always easy. The drawing below appeared in the *Dover Times* in November 1911. Under the sub-heading "Every picture tells a story" this is actually an advertisement for some kind of medication for aches and pains but the message is very clear – a mother's hands are always full, her worries never cease, and she never has time for looking after herself.

What Edwardian women wore
Edwardian fashions in East Kent

The August Bank Holiday used to be held on the first Monday of the month. In 1905 "The New Palace steamers brought thousands of visitors" down to Margate and "Never was the hatless brigade more in evidence." Thousands of visitors had "discarded their head gear" and allowed "their locks to float in the breeze".[6] Those were the days! The last comment is particularly interesting as in Edwardian England people normally wore hats and gloves in public, and wealthier ladies carried parasols to protect their pale complexions.

Queen's Promenade in Cliftonville in 1909

Gentlemen still wore collars and ties on the promenade but some wore white flannel trousers while on holiday. The reporter suggests that Londoners escaping from the metropolis could quite literally "let their hair down" when they arrived in Margate, but most visitors still dressed formally, whatever the weather! Only children were allowed to run around bare-legged. Postcards from the period often show the people on the cliff-tops holding on to their hats!

Harem and scarem!

This article describes the daring promenade of one young lady along the Leas at Folkestone in a harem skirt, which was divided skirt similar to *culottes*. The two sections covered the whole leg but were usually drawn in at the ankles.

A sensation was caused on the Leas on Sunday by the appearance of a young lady wearing a harem skirt. She walked along the promenade by the Upper Bandstand during the performance in the afternoon and attracted much attention. The trouser portion of the costume was of black, the remainder being of light blue material. The Lady also appeared at Sandgate in the afternoon, and at about eight o'clock reappeared on the Leas. "Church Parade" was in progress, the promenade being thronged with people.

The harem skirt again drew keen attention. Some regarded it with amusement, others with aversion, and others with derision. There were many shocked expressions at the lady's boldness, whilst others expressed their warm admiration at the lady's pluck, in committing such a violation of the sacred rules of conventionality. The wearer was accompanied by another lady and a gentleman, all of whom seated themselves near the Leas Bandstand. A crowd rapidly assembled. The party made a move in the direction of the Pleasure Gardens Theatre, and were followed by a large crowd of men, women and children. The men laughed, women hooted, whilst the rising generation sang such songs as "I wouldn't have a girl with a harem skirt."

The molested party made direct for the taxi-cab stand outside the Theatre, the crowd, continually increasing in size, following close behind. Eventually the party took refuge in a taxi-cab and drove off in the direction of the Railway Station. It is reported that the young lady comes from Ashford, and that she dared to promenade the Leas in a harem skirt for a wager.[7]

The photograph (*left*) shows a young woman in about 1912 in an outfit featuring a harem skirt that, apart from the hat, would still look very fashionable even today. A humorous postcard of the time showed a woman waving a women's rights banner being marched away by a policeman. The heading "The Scarem skirt" obviously refers to the harem skirt, but the woman depicted is older and frumpy and is wearing clumpy shoes and trousers underneath her skirt.

What Edwardian women wore

The little poem underneath hints at the old saying "you can tell who wears the trousers in their home".

> You've pinched my army
> You've pinched my ears
> You've disarranged our blouses
> But don't you dare to pinch my word!
> NOT IN THESE TROUSERS.

Women wearing trousers were understood to be the boss in their own households. This fashion for harem skirts did not last long at the time but during the First World War some women in the messier jobs did start to wear trousers at work.

Bobby's department store in Cliftonville

In Margate the main women's outfitters was Bobby's in Cecil Square. Bobby's opened their second store on the Northdown Road in Cliftonville in 1913, The building is still there today although now it is split into several different shops.

In Ramsgate there were several shops catering for ladies' every requirement, but perhaps the best known was Lewis, Hyland and Linom's in Harbour Street. The premises are now a haberdashery emporium, one of the finest in the country. Both stores also had branches in Folkestone, and other south coast towns. This was Lewis, Hyland and Linom's store in Rendezvous Street in Folkestone in January 1913 (*right*). Only the very wealthiest customers would have arrived by motor car!

In Dover, Florence Igglesden (From Bond Street) was exhibiting a "Special show of summer millinery"

Women in Kent

in Castle Street. "Cheap Knock-about Hats" were her speciality![8] F W Mann's store in Snargate Street specialized in blouses, while Percy Houlden's of Cannon Street offered "Perfect fitting Corsets" throughout 1910. Nora Murch of Castle Street offered French and English model dresses made up from two-and-a-half guineas!

Falconer and Sons in Dover and Deal were naval, military and ladies' tailors and in Canterbury women could shop at Lefevres or Hunts.

In 1907 in Ramsgate a Miss Corder advertised as a "high-class costumier and ladies' tailor" at No 4 York Terrace opposite the harbour.

The women's column in the local paper always had a fashion item. Sometimes they were practical tips such as how to remove stains but more often they described the latest London fashions.

The vogue for stripes!

> Alternately with the fashion for the wearing of plain fabrics there comes always a vogue for stripes, and it seems as though striped materials would assert themselves almost immediately and to a considerable extent. Striped cloths and striped tweeds, both in black and white and in colours, are already on the ascendant, and later in the season we shall undoubtedly see a good many striped silks and soft satins, as well as striped gauzes and chiffons for evening wear. Arranged with discretion and carried out with stripes that are not too wide, these fabrics are very becoming, as they give an elegant appearance of height to the figure and length and slimness to the waist.[9]

In an article about Paris fashions the *Thanet Times* points out that: "In Paris there are distinctly two types of women. On the one hand there is the severely neat tailor-made woman, while on the other we have the picturesque negligee pose, where the disposition is to droop from head to foot, and the significant features are a short waist, a long, tight, clinging skirt and the 'picture' hat."

So far as tailor-made gowns are concerned:

Many of these coats are made in dark tweeds, with two or more stripes in sober shades, and arranged with small vests in some quite pale contrasting tint. With tailor-made gowns a high linen collar is generally de rigueur, varied only by a soft lingerie cravat in fine cambric, with insertions of broderie-de-main edged with lace.

In the accompanying sketch we have a lovely tailor model. It is in a new cinnamon shade of faced cloth, with a skirt cut somewhat after the corselet style, and a fascinating little bolero of cloth is braided à l'Empire, with the faintest shade of gold and purple running through. The lingerie jabot is in finest cambric edged with Valenciennes. The fascinating picture hat in bottle-green felt, perched high on the head and trimmed with a swirling mass of osprey plumes.[10]

What Edwardian women wore

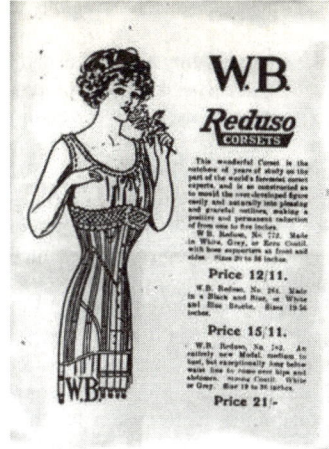

This article from *The Common Cause* in March 1910 shows that even suffragists were sometimes concerned with the vagaries of haute couture.

The 1910 Corset Crisis!

No mode of recent years has called for more subtle a change in the corset production than the spring 1910 fashion. A corset style making so exacting a demand upon the originality and resourcefulness of the corset designer should prove a veritable Gordian knot to the great mass of corsetieres. (Neat flat slide, not a clumsy buckle)[11]

The advertisement (*above left*) from *Votes for Women* in June 1911 from a salon in Kensington High Street gives some insight into how Edwardian women managed to maintain such a gorgeous figure. And this pose by an Edwardian actress (*above right*) shows the typical S-bend figure aspired to by most Edwardian women. The bodice was moulded on a tight and well-boned foundation garment. The narrow waist was accentuated by a waistband. In this photograph the woman has a charming chain link purse hanging from her waist. This skirt has more gathers but other slimmer skirts were deliberately given a concave shape curving inwards towards the knee and then curving out again at the hem, hiding all but the tips of the shoes. To accentuate this shape women often leant on a long-handled parasol or posed for a photograph leaning on a chair back, or as in this case an elaborate Edwardian fireplace. Sleeve styles varied but were usually tight for part of their length as in the leg-of-mutton style. Other sleeves were looser but gathered in at the cuff. Collars were usually high around the neck for daytime activities but necklines were more revealing for evening wear.

Tea gowns were also very popular as they were loose-fitting and comfortable, yet often elaborately trimmed or embroidered. Edith Nesbit, the children's author, was particularly fond of her Liberty tea gowns and used to wear them at home when she was writing at her desk.

Hobble skirts were said to have been designed by Paul Poiret after meeting Katherine Wright, the sister of Wilbur and Orville, who used to tie a rope round her legs to prevent her skirt getting in the way when she flew with her brothers. Needless to say the fashion, although very elegant, was short-lived as it was very impractical. Women could only take very small steps in a hobble skirt, and it was impossible to get in and out of cars, or most other forms of transport while wearing them. This delightful creation (*right*) comes complete with an enormous muff, perfect for hiding a hammer in!

Edwardian women were gradually trying a wide variety of sports too. Suitable clothes for enjoying games of tennis, croquet, cricket and golf were on offer. Women had always ridden horses but now they could cycle or travel in motor cars as well. In seaside towns many were joining swimming clubs. They needed more practical, less restrictive clothing in suitable fabrics. This advertisement (*below*) from a Thanet newspaper of 1909 shows how women still managed to look elegant and feminine whilst riding a bicycle, even when they had to hold on to their hats.

What Edwardian women wore
Autumnal fashions

Here, contrary to expectations, the tight skirt still prevails, and I for one rejoice that it is so. I do not speak of the "hobble" which has made such grand and gratuitous copy for Mr Punch – exaggerations are never *le vrai chic* – but of the stride-wide skirt, that refuses to get muddy, leaves both hands free, and packs into the space of a pocket handkerchief. Contrast it with its predecessor of five yards width, made to touch – sometimes to sweep the ground!

Now as to hats, well for the *occasion de cérémonie* they are still immense, but for everyday wear they are mercifully much smaller. In both instances simplicity with a *cachet* is the main endeavour. Picture a large black velvet hat lined with white and adorned only by an immense *boutonnière* of white kid roses.

If you would have your morning blouse *très correct* get a silk or wool stripe that repeats the colours of the tweed skirt that it is to be worn with. For more dressy occasions I saw some specially pretty and quite inexpensive delaine, silk and lace blouses at Hyams in Oxford Street. M. W.[12]

In September 1910 a fascinating article entitled 'The 1910 Female' written by a vicar on the Isle of Wight was re-printed in the *Kentish Gazette & Canterbury Press*. He writes, "For some weeks past we have enjoyed the presence of summer visitors . . ." but he continues "who devises their clothing?" He recalls the time when English girls were attractive and tasteful but now he says "the 1910 female seems to either be wrapped up in a bundle of rags, with the least clean one spread over her hat and tied under her chin, or else she discards as much clothing as she can. She leaves her hat at home and gets her head full of dust, exposes her chest to every wind that blows. Display ankles that show the solidity of her understanding, runs about (the island) half clad, crumpled and dust-laden." The vicar admits that "maybe we are getting old, and do not properly appreciate the spirit of the twentieth century" but he feels that the motorist is to blame for this deterioration in the standards of women's dress and resents the arrogant motorists who come "hooting, squeaking, bellowing, tinkling, roaring or whistling with a piercing scream to tell everybody to get out of the way because the road belongs to him".[13]

Bobby's of Folkestone were offering this streamlined sports costume in March 1913 for 49/11. A special feature of this costume was that the skirt buttoned up the entire length of the front and was consequently specially adapted for sports wear.[14]

In February 1911 the annual wait to see whether skirts would be wide or narrow, or coats short or long, was over. Beneath the headline "Slenderness still imperative", readers of the *Dover Times* were informed that "The straight lines that we have grown to admire," which made women look more youthful, were to stay, but skirts were to measure at least two yards around the hem so that "we shall be spared the ridiculous sights which caused so much amusement when the hobble craze was at its height". Coats were to be high-waisted and trimmed with braid, and narrow stripes were also fashionable during that season.[15] This delightful drawing accompanied the article. In the words of a popular song at the time "Where did you get that hat?"

A spring epidemic

In the spring of 1914 women were choosing between spotted fabrics and checks.

> During the last few years a spring epidemic of checks has been most prevalent, and this year the disease is going to be more than ever.
>
> Every sort of check from the tiniest shepherd's plaid to great draughtboard squares can be worn. Check dresses, check tailormades, check sports coats, check millinery, and check stockings are now filling the windows of all the West End shops, and very soon they will be filling the streets as well.
>
> They can be had (writes Helen Newton) in almost any colours, though black and white are by far the most popular. Simple little black frocks of black and white check, with sashes of brightly coloured flowered silk, look charming for children and young girls and for morning wear. I greatly like the untrimmed tailormades in check, but for the girl who has to make her spring frock or tailormade last throughout the summer I would strongly advise her to choose something other than checks. If she can cast it aside in three months then the sooner she buys a check suit the better, but not otherwise. Plaids, too, in the most wonderful and striking colour mixtures are among other spring invaders, but most of these are too extraordinary to become in any sense popular."[16]

Two weeks later the fashion page of the *Thanet Times* contained the following:

> Spotted materials are among the rivals to the checks and plaids for waistcoats and tunic edgings.

What Edwardian women wore

Delightful lace scarves are edged around with ostrich feathering of two or three shades of one colour.

Pretty shopping hats are of the sailor variety with narrow brims and soft crowns. Some of these crowns, which just fit the head, widen out until at the top, where the stiff crown band of ribbon terminates, they are about of the same circumference as the brims

Vivid and large poinsettias make the splash of colour on big hats of black or *tête de nêgre*. The fine straw or moire covered shape will twist its big brim up at the left, or at the back, and beneath its shadow will be perched the flowers of red.

Little square buttons covered with silks are ranged in groups on blouse sleeves and fronts. Some shaped hip yokes, below which tunics fall in fullness, have these sets of squares at the front and at the back.[17]

Waistcoats for women

The cape and the waistcoat are the two all-conquering heroes in the dress world this season (says Helen Newton in *The Daily News*). The one or the other, or both, are seen on almost every toilette of a fashionable order, and the designs are so infinitely varied that it should not be difficult to get a style that is becoming to every figure, no matter what its height or its breadth may be.

Both fashions are exceedingly picturesque, but the waistcoats are particularly so, as all the great artists have long ago discovered.

In the pictures by Raeburn, Van Dyck, Rubens, Gainsborough, Romney and Reynolds many styles of waistcoats will be found, and the modern ones are mostly modelled on these beautiful examples.

Plain silks, striped silks, and flowered silks are all used for the elaborate waistcoat, but for wearing with plain morning tailormades there is nothing to equal the waistcoat of spotless white pique, with its high outstanding collar of the same material.

An altogether original dress of black and white taffetas had a quaint white pique waistcoat, which fastened with one big button in the centre of the front, and fell into long points over the waistband.

The collar was cut in one with the waistcoat, and spread out at each side in gigantic points. This costume was almost entirely of white taffetas, the black and white striped silk forming the tunic and trimming the edge of the neat little bolero.[18]

Suffragette colours

In June 1913 many department stores, such as Swan and Edgar's at Piccadilly Circus in London, were offering "Serviceable attire at moderate prices" and "Hats trimmed with ribbon in NU colours" for women taking part in the national suffrage pilgrimage.[19]

Suffragettes were able to buy a huge variety of souvenirs and fashion accessories in the WSPU's colours of purple, white and green. These were advertised in *Votes for Women* and sold at leading department stores as well as at WSPU shops. Motor scarves, ties and badges were popular but there were also hatpins and handkerchiefs.

Women in Kent

Emmeline Pethick-Lawrence explained the WSPU colours, which had been chosen for the Hyde Park demo in June 1908, in the 1909 programme for the WSPU exhibition which was held at the Prince's skating rink. White was for purity 'in public as well as private life', green stood for hope and purple for dignity, although it was sometimes said to stand for loyalty or courage. Green was also supposed to stand for youth or regeneration.

The NUWSS colours were red and white in 1907 and 1908 but in November 1909 *The Common Cause* announced the decision to add green. Members were asked to try really hard to display the colours at every opportunity.

White – the supreme faith in ideas which makes the soul divine

Green – the perpetual re-florescence of hope and youth into the fruit of well-doing

Red – the passion and the blood of martyrs and heroes[20]

During the First World War, of course, many women were going to work outside the home so clothes became simpler and more practical. Many women were in any case wearing uniforms or protective clothing at work as safety was also an issue. By 1918 skirts and coats were above the ankles, plainer and mainly in darker, more serviceable colours. This was partly out of respect for all the families that were grieving, but was also an economic necessity.

By the time all women in Britain got the vote in 1928 most women were dressed like this in simple cloche hats, calf-length skirts and wrapover coats as can be seen from these photos of my respective grandmothers. Many of these clothes would have been home-made.

My paternal grandmother (*left*) is sitting on Ramsgate harbour wall wearing shiny lisle stockings and laced-up walking shoes. My maternal grandmother (*opposite page*, wearing glasses) is walking down Sandgate Road in Folkestone with her sister. My aunt is in the pram and my mother, then aged six, is walking along beside them.

It is interesting to note that, while all the women have the new shorter hairstyles, my mother had long ringlets. These were wrapped round rags at night. She was not allowed to cut her hair until she was sixteen years old, and had started her first job. She came home one day and presented her mother with her two long plaits. Needless to say her mother was not amused!

What Edwardian women wore

[1] TT 27th June 1913
[2] VW 17th November 1911
[3] TT 30th June 1913
[4] TT 14th April 1905
[5] EKT 17th April 1907
[6] TT 11th August 1905
[7] FH 15th July 1911
[8] DE 8th July 1910
[9] EKT 30th January 1907
[10] TT 8th January 1908
[11] CC 3rd March 1910
[12] VW 21st October 1910
[13] KGCP 10th September 1910
[14] FH 22nd March 1913
[15] DTEKG 29th February 1911
[16] TT 6th March 1914
[17] TT 20th March 1914
[18] TT 5th June 1914
[19] CC 20th June 1913
[20] CC 26th May 1910

Chapter Four

Early days in the struggle

> As this is not a party question, nor a class question, so neither is it a sex question. I have no fear lest the woman should encroach upon the power of the man. The fear I have is, lest we should invite her unwittingly to trespass upon the delicacy, the purity, the refinement, the elevation of her own nature, which are the present sources of its power. (William Ewart Gladstone on female suffrage in 1892)

In the 1860s several Kentish towns such as Folkestone and Tunbridge Wells presented petitions to Parliament asking for women's suffrage. Ramsgate was the second Kentish town to present a petition on 18th February 1869, followed by another three years later on 2nd May 1872.

Apart from the usual household tips and the occasional recipe, fashion articles accounted for most of the copy on the women's page of the local paper in the early years of the twentieth century. By 1905, however, reports of some meetings where women's issues were being discussed began to appear.

On Friday 3rd February 1905, the Margate Women's Liberal and Progressive Association held a meeting in the Foresters Hall, Margate at 8pm. The speaker was Miss Florence Balgarnie who spoke on "Some Political Lessons from our Australian and New Zealand Colonies".

Florence Balgarnie from Folkestone had been campaigning for women's suffrage since the 1880s. She had recently returned from a sixteen-month trip to the colonies and reported on the "land question" and fiscal reform. Some states in Australia and New Zealand had already given women the vote, and it was mainly as a result of women having the vote that the number of public houses was decreasing. Her Margate audience applauded loudly on hearing this.

The relation of women to the state

At a meeting of the Margate Pioneer Society in 1905, Mrs D H Macfarlane, a Poor Law Guardian, gave a most interesting and instructive paper on "The Relation of Women to the State". She spoke about women as citizens and how their interests were identical with those of men.

> Privileges were vouchsafed to citizens on certain conditions, and all citizens fulfilling these conditions should reap the reward. But as women knew only too well, such was not the case, and there was an increasing tendency in all fresh local government measures to impose fresh disabilities on women. Women had made great strides in education during the past few years, and there were women workers in almost every department of life – even Government offices had opened their doors, and factories and schools had their women inspectors, and their work of public usefulness had been proved and not found wanting. Therefore the principle having been conceded that their work might be a helpful contribution to that of men – hopes were raised

that their co-operation would have been welcomed and looked upon as a "sine qua non". But the reverse was the case. Certain laws are laid down by men disabling women to perform any active service as a citizen, though she may pay rates and taxes just the same as men. For instance – no woman could sit on County Councils, and if an Urban District Council became a Corporation, the right of a woman to sit was lost.

Mrs Macfarlane then quoted Lord Hobhouse who had said that "we are by our refusals to employ women in public functions guilty of a waste of power almost incredibly stupid".

A draper's shop in Ramsgate High Street in about 1912

She went on to say that

> Some people wondered why women wanted the franchise. They wanted it for the same reason that men wanted it – because nothing could be done without it. It was the key that unlocked the door to all reforms – to all legislation for whatsoever class it was needed, and "no taxation without representation" should apply to women as well as men. Many foolish and narrow-minded objections were raised why women should not have the vote, but, seeing that women were proving themselves capable and devoted citizens, were exercising the local franchise – serving on public bodies – were paying taxes and contributions to the State, and were amenable to the laws of the land they had every right to vote the same as the men.[1]

By April 1906 Thanet newspapers began to report regularly on the behaviour and tactics used by the suffragists in London who believed that they had to make themselves unpleasant to achieve their goal. During one of Mr Keir Hardie's speeches for woman suffrage: " . . a scene occurred almost unparalleled in the history of Parliament: a speaker was interrupted by cheers and shouts from the

Early Days in the Struggle

Ladies' Gallery" and "a flag was thrust through the grille and waved at the assembly, bearing the legend: Votes for Women".[2]

This emotional account of women's struggle for enfranchisement appeared in January 1907.

> Anyone strolling up High-street at half past ten on Monday evening last would have met a band of mute, sad-eyed women wandering homeward, weary at heart. And no wonder! The stern voice of the local parliament has denied them, at any rate for a time, that precious privilege yet to be rendered to their all-conquering claims –the right to vote.[3]

I think this is referring to Broadstairs, but all of Thanet's High Streets are on hills so it is difficult to be sure!

This tongue-in-cheek article appeared in March 1907:

> The Ramsgate municipal reformers must have a care or they will bring down on their heads the wrath of the female suffragettes. Last night, at the meeting in West Central Ward, a chivalrous and noble champion of the dames proposed that the ladies should be eligible for election on the committee of the Reform Association. He pointed out that many ladies in the town were occupiers of houses and municipal voters, and argued from that fact that the ladies were entitled to be heard on any subject that related to the good government of the town. His course was good, his logic unanswerable, but will you believe me ladies, when I tell you, that out of that great assembly of men he found only one supporter in his appeal for a consideration of your rights? I expect the women of Ramsgate to rise up in their wrath and slay someone. The secretaries of the Association are – No! I will not betray them.[4]

At a Liberal Party meeting in Broadstairs in April Alderman W Thompson of Richmond spoke in favour of Women's Suffrage. He said that where it had been tried in New Zealand and Australia none of the terrible things that were predicted had happened. He added that: "Women would no doubt do many silly things, (Laughter) but they could not do anything sillier than the men who returned the last Tory Government to power. (Applause)"[5]

An article re-printed from the *Lady's Pictorial* in July 1907 asked whether it was unreasonable to deny women the vote since they have proved beyond doubt that they can "deal with political questions quite as clearly, and perhaps far more convincingly than many male campaigners". A former prime minister had acknowledged that "the modern lady canvasser no longer relies on personal charms and pretty gowns, but on her sound knowledge of the subject", and that she understood politics "far better than nine-tenths of the men whose votes she secures for parliamentary candidates".[6]

In October 1907 the question of whether ladies should be admitted to meetings was being considered by the Isle of Thanet Debating Society. It was decided that ladies could be admitted to the ladies' gallery on presentation of members' cards endorsed by the Secretary, but the Society was, however, "ungallant enough to reject a proposition that ladies be admitted as members".[7]

Thanet Times, *31st March 1905*

---

[1] TT 3rd November 1905
[2] IOTG 28th April 1906
[3] EKT 23rd January 1907
[4] EKT 27th March 1907
[5] EKT 17th April 1907
[6] EKT 17th July 1907
[7] EKT 16th October 1907

Chapter Five

Anti-suffrage activity in East Kent

The Queen is most anxious to enlist everyone in checking this mad, wicked folly of "Women's Rights", with all its attendant horrors on which her poor sex is bent. It is a subject which makes the Queen so furious that she cannot contain herself. (Queen Victoria in 1870)

Arguments against female enfranchisement

It is hardly surprising that the majority of those opposing woman suffrage were men, but what is perhaps more surprising is that a large number of women, led by Queen Victoria, were also against giving women the vote.

Barbara Leigh Smith Bodichon, herself a suffragist, listed as the main arguments given against woman suffrage:

- Women do not want the vote.
- Women have other duties.

Barbara Bodichon argued that "some women do want votes" as the petitions women had signed proved, but "unless we could poll the women" which was "the very measure under discussion" it was not possible to say whether they were in the majority. She suggested that once registration of women electors was made possible they would soon see "how many care to avail themselves of the privilege". She also argued that "it is very true that women have other duties – many and various. But so have men. No citizen lives for his citizen duties only."

Other reasons given against woman suffrage were:

- Women were financially dependent on men, therefore not entitled to the same rights.
- A female electorate would be vulnerable to reactionary influences.
- There might be damage to women's nervous dispositions if they took part in the rough and tumble of electioneering at the hustings.
- Giving women rights was a danger to national security as it might send the wrong message to colonies and rivals such as Germany.
- Women who could vote would gain more influence in the public sphere and take jobs away from men.
- Women were not admitted into the Church, the Army or the Navy. It was men's business to fight and women's business to look after the home. If women could not enforce the law physically they were not allowed to vote.

On this last point Frances Power Cobbe,, in her "Address to Women Concerning the Suffrage", argued in 1874 that women had used up all the "weapons of ratiocinative warfare" and that "Had Logic been the only obstacle in our way, we should long ago have been polling our votes." She continued "to the ever-recurring charge that we cannot fight, and therefore ought not to vote, we have replied that the logic of the exclusion will be made manifest when all the men too weak, too short or too old for the military standard be likewise disfranchised, and when the actual soldiers of our army are accorded the suffrage". Frances Cobbe also warned that the greatest obstacle to achieving woman suffrage lay with "idle women – the wives of rich men who have never known a want unsupplied, who have been surrounded by tenderness and homage from their cradles".

She was probably thinking about the sort of women who signed Mrs Humphrey Ward's "Appeal against Female Suffrage" which was printed in the *Nineteenth Century* review magazine in 1889. Readers were asked to fill in a petition form and return it to the editor. Mrs Humphrey Ward claimed that "the pursuit of a mere outward equality with men is for women not only vain but demoralizing. It leads to a total misconception of women's true dignity and special mission." Among those who signed her petition were several duchesses and viscountesses and fifteen "Ladies", including Lady Randolph Churchill.

Opposition to "Votes for Women" in East Kent

In the *Thanet Advertiser* of 3rd March 1907 Ermine K Taylor, Honorary Secretary of the Woman's Anti-Suffrage Movement in London wrote to ask if any local lady in Ramsgate would administer a branch of the anti-suffrage movement.

The Women's National Anti-Suffrage League was founded in 1908, with its own newspaper, *The Anti-Suffrage Review*. By 1914 the League had some 42,000 subscribers and another 15,800 sympathisers – almost as many as the NUWSS.

A few weeks earlier, this poem attributed to Callie Bonnie Marble appeared in *Keble's Gazette*.

A little anti-suffragist

My mamma is looking for rights, dolly, and running for office they say
I think woman suffrage is dreadful, when it takes our mammas away
And a mamma can't be a papa, if she does wear his collars and ties
And I'd rather she'd just be my mamma, than ever and ever so wise
And Papa feels just as we do, I heard some words that he said
When a woman forgets she's a woman, her husband had better be dead
It may be very progressive, I hear that again and again
But I cannot help wondering, dolly, what will become of the men?

In a letter to the editor of the *Thanet Times* about "Women's Suffrage", Lucy M Garnett, an anti-suffragist, quotes the late Mrs Henry Fawcett who said "That women are not unfitted, by reason of their sex, from forming an opinion on political questions." The writer discusses the characteristic mental and moral differences between the sexes claiming that: "Intellectually, women are more desultory and volatile than men, more occupied with particular instances than with general principles, and prone to judge rather by intuitive perception than by deliberate reasoning or the results of experience."[1]

An Anti-Suffrage League branch was established at Ramsgate in 1909 at Southwood House, the home of Lady Rose Weigall. The principal speaker was Miss Dickens, a grand-daughter of the great novelist. Mrs Jane Welby Pugin, widow of the illustrious architect Augustus Pugin, also attended the meeting but died a few weeks later.[2]

Anti-suffrage activity in East Kent

The manifesto of the Women's National Anti-Suffrage League was read out at a meeting in St John's Hall in Margate:

1. It is time that the women who are opposed to the concession of the parliamentary franchise to women should make themselves fully and widely heard. The arguments on the other side have been put with great ability and earnestness, in season and out of season, and enforced by methods legitimate and illegitimate.
2. An Anti-Suffrage League has therefore been formed, and all women who sympathise with its objects are earnestly requested to join it.

Paragraph (5) states the main reason why this league opposes the concession of the parliamentary vote to women, the first three reasons are as follows:

a) Because the spheres of men and women, owing to natural causes, are essentially different, and therefore their share in the public management of the State should be different.

b) Because the complex modern State depends for its existence on naval and military power, diplomacy, finance, and the great mining, constructive, shipping and transport industries, in none of which can women take any practical part. Yet it is upon these matters, and the vast interests involved in them, that the work of Parliament turns.

c) Because by the concession of the local government vote and the admission of women to County and Borough Councils the nation has opened a wide sphere of public work and influence to women, which is within their powers. To make proper use of it, however, will tax all the energies that women have to spare, apart from the care of the home and the development of the individual life.

Miss Weigall, who became Honorary Secretary of the branch, moved a vote of thanks to Lady Bancroft for presiding, and mentioned that the Thanet Branch of the League was formed eight weeks ago. It had a membership of over 60, and over 1,200 signatures had been obtained to the petition against the suffrage. Hitherto the branch's work had been almost exclusively confined to Ramsgate.[3]

No votes for women

The first annual meeting of the Women's National Anti-Suffrage League was held in London on 21st June 1909. There were 95 branches in the United Kingdom, with a membership of over 9,000.[4] The first annual report of the Thanet Branch of the Women's Anti-Suffrage League, which was founded on 1st February 1909, stated that the branch had 81 members and 1,496 names had been sent from Thanet on a petition to Parliament on 1st March 1909. Both parliamentary candidates in the Thanet elections, Mr Weigall and Mr Craig, declared themselves against women's suffrage.[5]

In the Congregational Hall in Ramsgate on Wednesday 27th April 1910 a meeting of the Women's Anti-Suffrage League was held. The speaker Mrs Archibald Colquhoun used her speech to reply to the arguments advanced by Mrs Pankhurst in her speech at Ramsgate the previous week. At the close of her address the speaker was cordially applauded. There were a good many questions, which Mrs Colquhoun ably dealt with, and a gentleman who was rather persistent in his queries was gently but firmly sat upon.[6]

Women in Kent

Ramsgate beach near the harbour wall

> *Ethel Colquhoun was an anti-feminist. Wife of the explorer and travel writer Archibald Colquhoun, she wrote several books including The Vocation of Women published by Macmillan in London in 1913.*

When Mrs Pankhurst spoke in Dover in October 1910 she addressed the anti-suffragists in the audience by claiming that: "The only justification for their agitation against women's suffrage was that they should carry out at the same time a vigorous agitation to relieve women from payment of taxes." She was well aware that this was impossible as the state could not do without the money women contributed.[7]

The Dean of Canterbury, Dr Wace presided over a meeting of the Canterbury branch of the National Anti-Woman Suffrage League in January 1911. One of the speakers was Mr Arnold Ward MP, son of the well-known novelist and anti-suffragist, Mrs Humphrey Ward. He spoke mostly about the weakness of women!

In summing up, the Dean expressed the widely held view of anti-suffragists, that, as women were excluded from the Church, the Army and the Navy, they should be excluded from political action as well. He added that:

> ... up to the present time, it has been the man's business to fight, and it has been the women's business to look after the home, to educate the children, and to sweeten and soften the character of the men. Mix them up together, let the woman come into the fighting ranks, and that softening influence is gone for ever.[8]

The front cover of *The Common Cause* of 17th November 1910 has a delightful drawing of very fashionably dressed ladies wearing hobble skirts. The heading reads: "A vision of Fair Ladies, as seen by the Anti-Suffrage Press". The conversation goes as follows:

First Fair One: A Vote? How silly! I can twist any voter round my little finger.

Anti-suffrage activity in East Kent

Second Fair One: Oh! Please do tell me. What is a vote?

Third Fair One: What does she mean by talking about women's wages, when the far more anxious question of men's wages is still unsettled.

Fourth Fair One: Why add to women's burdens the intolerable burden of the vote.

Fifth Fair One: Those dreadful women! I must call Archie to protect me.

Sixth Fair One: Most unwomanly! Why women could not even walk to the vote! [*This last was a reference to the hobble skirts which were almost impossible to walk in.*]

To an anti-suffragist

You ask me to listen to the noise of shattered glass and to condemn the breakers
Ah, friend, I cannot hear it for the sound of the wailing of outraged children
You point me to the ruins of burnt houses, but I cannot see them
For my eyes are running over with tears for my sweated sister, half-starved, bending over her work
You show me a few blackened letters, and I ask you for an accounting of the little human messages lost every year to protected vice.
You talk of wire-cutting and spoiled turf, and I ask you this question:
Why is a child's lost innocence, a child's marred body of less importance to a judge in a Christian land than damaged property?
I see everywhere about me wretchedness, unnecessary poverty, misrule, tyranny, lust and dishonour,
And I know that had women a voice much of this evil might be overcome;
Yet you ask me to blame violent protest on the part of the women of England,
I say to you, O blind one, O weak one, O cowardly one
I say it not only to you, but I shout it to the world
I shout it to the great Heaven where God watches
Is there no wilder cry, no fiercer fight? Is there no stronger weapon?
Give it into our hand, O God of battles.[9]

Almon Hensley

Sophia Almon Hensley was born in Nova Scotia in 1866 but was educated in England and Paris. Her first book of poetry was published privately in 1889, the year she married the Halifax lawyer Hubert Hensley. She became a popular speaker at women's meetings. Some of her finest poetry was written about the home-front experience during the First World War.

Election lunacy

In March 1905 the *Isle of Thanet Gazette* re-printed this gem which originally appeared in the *Daily Mirror*:

> Dr Forbes Winslow, the eminent brain specialist claimed that women risk their sanity by indulging in politics and that "The General Election is a serious menace to the sanity of the country."
>
> "It will", he says, "be far better for England when the general election is over. Many people, whose highly strung nervous temperaments have been affected by the political excitement will find their minds unhinged – some temporarily, some permanently. The asylums will find themselves inundated by weak-minded people whose minds have given way under the strain, and who will proclaim themselves Balfours, Chamberlains, Churchills and John Burnses."

Women in Kent

Dr Forbes Winslow reserved his most solemn warning for women politicians. "It is impossible to over-estimate the injurious and pernicious effect of the excitement of politics upon a women's brain. With men it is bad enough: with women it is ten times worse. What mother, what wife, what sister wishes to lose her reason, to wreck her life, for the sake of a fortnight's hysterical effort for the "cause?" And that is what politics for ladies may very easily mean."

Dr Forbes Winslow feared that political excitement would result in "violent mania, ambitious monomania, and melancholia", and he educated masses would be those chiefly affected."[10]

A *Punch* cartoon in January 1906 hinted at this election hysteria. A sensible women replies to a "shrieking sister" that far from "helping our cause" she was "its worst enemy".[11]

There were a lot of references in the newspapers and periodicals of the day to women's nervous dispositions or debilitated constitutions! Woman's frailty as the weaker sex and her weak and fragile constitution are often referred to by male reporters. This discreet advertisement for cure-all "Female Pills" appeared in the *Thanet Times* in March 1905, but there is no clue as to what the pills contained![12]

> **Dr. Davis's famous Female Pills**
> Have been universally admitted to be a boon to Womankind
>
> They are the best known remedy for Anaemia, Giddiness, Fulness [*sic!*] and Swelling after Meals, Loss of Appetite, Hysteria, Palpitation of the Heart, Debility, Depression, Weakness, Irregularities, and all Female ailments. May be had from Chemists and Patent Medicine Vendors everywhere, or from the Proprietor.

In her article on "The Restlessness of Modern Woman", Mrs C Humphry wonders if

> . . . some, at least, of the mischief may not be caused by the incessant restlessness of modern life." For many women, she argues "Excitement is the best-liked mental food in many lives. A frothy hubbub fills the days that might be spent in a delightful leisure of congenial occupation. It would seem to be a necessity to be always going somewhere and doing something. There are women who cannot face the prospect of an evening spent alone. To them there is something appalling in the idea of solitude." But she claims "without some chart of life's voyage we have no sure anchorage. We drift; we never have been taught to steer." She had observed that few women could "sit reposefully in these restless days. The majority fidget in their seats, re-arrange their draperies, change their attitude every five minutes, pat their back hair, push their veils out with their lips (a peculiarly ungainly habit)."[13]

Feminists already distrusted the medical profession because it had been such a struggle for women to be accepted and allowed to train and qualify as doctors. They felt that most men were only too happy to support any eminent doctor who offered a convincing medical explanation as to why women should not take part in the political arena.

In her book, *Marriage is a Trade,* published in 1909, Cicely Hamilton mentions a recent speech in which John Burns the Independent Labour MP was still telling school-girls that their mission, duty and livelihood was "To keep house, cook, nurse and delight in making others happy."

Anti-suffrage activity in East Kent

John Burns was a trade unionist who had taken part in the London Dock Strike of 1889. He was elected onto the newly formed London County Council as the member for Battersea in South London. In 1892, John Burns was elected to Parliament as the Independent Labour Party member for Battersea.

Cicely Hamilton believed that "the narrowing down of woman's hopes and ambitions to the sole pursuit and sphere of marriage" prevented women from diverting their energy into other channels. Most men still saw women as "incomplete" until taken in hand by a man.[14]

Hysteria was caused by conflict but the anti-suffragists argued that the conflict was brought about when women took part in activities not suitable for a women's physiological make-up, whereas the suffragists claimed it was the exclusion of women from active participation in political and social activities as an equal member of society which caused the conflict.

In the new field of psychoanalysis, Sigmund Freud had set out to prove that hysteria was essentially a feminine neurosis, and Almroth Wright, who was an eminent immunologist, based his anti-suffragist views on this claim that women are potentially or innately hysterical.

A report of a NUWSS meeting in Canterbury talks about the controversial book *The Unexpurgated Case against Women's Suffrage*, by Sir Almroth E Wright, published by Constable in 1913. The chairman of the meeting thought that "the author must be in private life somewhat of a humorist because he had made the purport of his attack upon the movement of such an extreme and exaggerated character that really it was hardly possible to take him quite seriously".[15]

Mrs Walter Gallichan spoke in 1913 at Caxton Hall on "Woman in her Relationship to man". She said that many of them had been reading Sir Almroth Wright's new book in which they were told that women were insolvent citizens, incapable of physical effort, of clear thinking, or of moral perception. Sir Almroth Wright MD FRS had done them real service. She wished women would own up to their real thoughts about the other sex as Sir Almroth had done. No book, for example, that she had ever read about women had taught her so much about men. She felt that nobody could possibly read Sir Almroth's indictment of women and mistake its significance. It was a modern expression of the age-old struggle between the two sexes. Man was disturbed and damaged by woman's new claims – he feared her, and through her he feared himself. So Sir Almroth had fastened his antagonism upon woman in emphatic and remorseless denunciation of what he considered her retarded development.[16] The following extract gives a flavour of what Mrs Gallichan spoke about:

Woman's Disability in the Matter of Intellect

The woman voter would be pernicious to the State not only because she could not back her vote by physical force, but also by reason of her intellectual defects.

Woman's mind attends in appraising a statement primarily to the mental images which it evokes, and only secondarily – and sometimes not at all – to what is predicated in the statement. It is over-influenced by individual instances; arrives at conclusions on incomplete evidence; has a very imperfect sense of proportion; accepts the congenial as true, and rejects the uncongenial as false; takes the imaginary which is desired for reality, and treats the undesired reality which is out of sight as non-existent.

On page 71 of his book, Sir Almroth had written: "The failure to recognize that man is the master, and why he is the master, lies at the root of the suffrage movement."

Catherine Gasquoine Hartley had published her own book, *The Truth about Women*, in 1913. She claimed that: "My book is a statement of my faith in Woman as the predominant and responsible partner in the relations of the sexes." She resigned her position as headmistress at Babington House School in Kent in 1903 to begin a career as a writer of non-fiction in London. Her first marriage was to Walter M Gallichan, himself a writer of some repute on psychoanalysis and women's issues.

In March 1914 Mrs Humphrey Ward, the famous novelist, who was always one of the keenest opponents of woman suffrage, was trying to set up a "grand council" of women with a network of local committees, which many were describing as a women's unofficial parliament or "House of Ladies sitting in Westminster Palace".

It was hoped that the "grand council" would be consulted by the Government of the day and would consist of ladies nominated by Mrs Ward, and would sit permanently at Westminster "to ponder over all Bills or Motions relating to women and children, to draft amendments, or even to initiate new Parliamentary action on all such questions as are fit for the female intelligence".[17]

Although the scheme was supposed to include suffragists and anti-suffragists, most suffragist organizations had not been told about it in advance!

The Anti-Suffrage League in 1914 had some 42,000 subscribers and another 15,800 sympathisers. With the Kaiser threatening Britain's Empire, female suffrage was seen by some as a danger to national security.

---

[1] TT 8th April 1908
[2] TT 3rd February 1909
[3] TT 7th April 1909
[4] TT 7th July 1909
[5] EKT 1st April 1910
[6] TT 23rd April 1910
[7] DE 28th October 1910
[8] KGCP 28th January 1911
[9] VW 13th June 1913
[10] IOTG 20th January 1906
[11] Punch 17th January 1906
[12] TT 3rd March 1905
[13] IOTG 6th January 1906
[14] *Marriage is a Trade*, 1909
[15] KGCP 22nd November 1913
[16] TT 13th October 1913
[17] TT 6th March 1914

Chapter Six

1908–1909

> Freedom! Citizenship! And the way to all that – the way to everything – is the vote!! (Kitty Brett in Chapter 10, *Ann Veronica* (1909) by HG Wells – who lived in Spade House (now called Wells House) in Sandgate 1898–1910.)

1908

On 18th January 1908 two suffragettes chained themselves to the railings outside No. 10 Downing Street. It took the police quite a while to release the women who were then taken to Cannon Row Police Station.

On 19th March 1908 in the Royal Albert Hall Christabel Pankhurst said: "It is because we are recognised today as women who are ready to act that the movement stands where it stands now."

Two days before the Hyde Park suffrage demonstration planned for 21st June 1908, MPs having tea on the terrace of the House of Commons were astonished to see a steam launch sail past full of suffragists waving banners to advertise their meeting.

June 21st was a beautiful summer's day when over 30,000 women, most in white gowns and flower-trimmed hats, processed to Hyde Park from all different directions. Eighty women speakers urged the women present to join them in their campaign by selling newspapers and carrying sandwich boards in parades to advertise meetings.

Marches with banners and brass bands were very much a part of the Edwardian scene both in England and on the continent, especially in Germany. The Mitchell and Kenyon short films taken mostly in the north of England during the first few years of the twentieth century give us tantalising silent glimpses of some of these processions. In the days before wireless and television, marches and rallies provided free entertainment for the masses, either as participants or as onlookers. Even very tiny children were dressed up in their finery for the annual Sunday School parade, and the growth of the Boys' Brigade and the Scout movement gave boys their chance to show off too. No-one could foresee that in a few years' time the women would be lining the streets proudly waving goodbye and cheering these same boys as they marched to the station en route for the poppy fields of Flanders.

Some of the parades went on for up to two hours but people tended to walk much more in those days. Many working-class families could not afford the luxury of a tram ride. Trades Unions, Temperance Societies and, later, the suffragists took to the streets to parade their loyalty to a particular society or cause. Historical tableaux on horse-drawn floats were popular, as were Clarion Vans which went round distributing socialist literature. No procession was complete without at least one brass band and, of course, there were the banners, usually strung between two poles and carried by two or more people. These were beautiful works of art, the result of hours of hard work by women. They were a mixture of appliqué, painted silk and embroidery. There are some good examples at the People's Museum in Manchester and the Women's Library in Whitechapel.

> A banner is not a literary affair, it is not a placard: leave such to boards and sandwichmen. A banner is a thing to float in the wind, to flicker in the breeze, to flirt its colours for your pleasure, to half show and half conceal a device you long to unravel: you do not want to read it, you want to worship it.

This quote from Mary Lowndes, member of the Artists' Suffrage League and designer of banners, appeared in the *English Woman*, September 1910.

On 30th June, when suffragettes were prevented by the police from reaching the Houses of Parliament, the first stones of the campaign were thrown at the windows of No. 10 Downing Street.

During the summer of 1908 Miss Muriel Matters from the NUWSS spoke at a garden party held at the home of Mrs Teetgen in Westgate-on-Sea. The object of the gathering was to introduce the suffrage question to the people of Westgate and to increase membership of the Margate branch of the NUWSS.

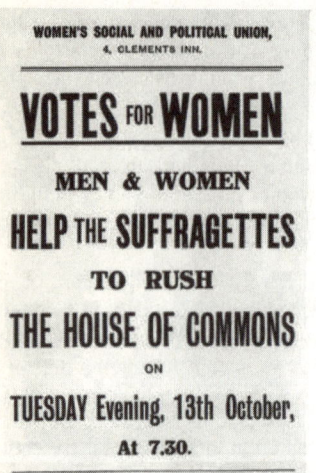

On 11th October 1908 Emmeline and Christabel Pankhurst and Flora Drummond addressed a crowd in Trafalgar Square inviting them to "Rush the House of Commons" the following Tuesday evening. Twenty-four women were arrested on that occasion, including Emmeline Pankhurst, who was imprisoned for the first time.

In November 1908 a Margate Pioneer Society meeting discussed the topic "Woman Suffrage". The speaker, Mrs Hicks of the Women's Freedom League, addressed a large audience. Mr Thornton Bobby, a well-known local businessman, was in the chair and gave a short resumé of the situation from a man's point of view. The speaker gracefully alluded to the chairman's broad-minded views, which she said, resembled those of Gladstone, who once said: "It is not for the Government of a country to wait until the majority ask for a Reform, but it is for us as statesmen and politicians, to anticipate their needs." Mrs Hicks claimed that the different organisations fighting for the removal of the sex-disability from the franchise had openly declared war on the Government. Other means having been exhausted during the last forty years, it rested with the Government to bring these unruly proceedings to a close. It is a lie, she continued, to say that these women go to prison for notoriety. It is "for the wrongs that need resistance, for the weak who need assistance, for the future in the distance, for the good that they may do". Mrs Hicks said she had never heard one valid reason, why she herself, who had paid taxes for twenty-five years, should not have a vote.[1]

1909

The WSPU are NOT asking for a vote for every women, but simply that sex shall cease to be a disqualification for the franchise.| (*Votes for Women*, 8th October 1909)

In Dover in February, 400 people, mostly women, attended an NUWSS meeting. Speakers included four women doctors – Dr Flora Murray and Dr Louisa Garrett Anderson among them.[2]

Helena Swanwick, a Manchester suffragist, who had been writing articles and book reviews for the *Manchester Guardian*, became editor of the NUWSS weekly journal *The Common Cause*.

Thanet whispers:

Why women want the vote – Well there are lots of reasons – but we admit that those given by Mrs Snowden at Margate on Friday were amongst the best – we see that the lady closed her able speech with a quotation – From Tennyson's epic "The Princess" – quotations are all very well - but why didn't the lady quote the next line?

> For Woman is not undevelopt man,
> But diverse: could we make her as the man,
> Sweet love were slain: his dearest bond is this,
> Not like to like, but like in difference.
> Yet in the long years liker must they grow;
> The man be more of woman, she of man;
> He gain in sweetness and in moral height,
> Nor lose the wrestling thews that throw the world;
> She mental breadth, nor fail in childward care,
> Nor lose the childlike in the larger mind;
> Till at the last she set herself to man,
> Like perfect music unto noble words;
> And so these twain, upon the skirts of Time,
> Sit side by side, full-summed in all their powers,
> Dispensing harvest, sowing the To-be,
> Self-reverent each and reverencing each,
> Distinct in individualities,
> But like each other even as those who love.
> Then comes the statelier Eden back to men:
> Then reign the world's great bridals, chaste and calm:
> Then springs the crowning race of humankind.
> May these things be![3]

The next line was: "Sighing she spoke 'I fear they will not.'"

Middle-class women who had been educated at good schools since the 1870s would have been familiar with this extremely long and tedious poem. The section which is usually quoted in the context of anti-suffrage is:

> Man for the field and woman for the hearth;
> Man for the sword and for the needle she;
> Man with the head, and woman with the heart;
> Man to command, and woman to obey;
> All else confusion.

Women in Kent

Why women should have the vote

I always like to be on the side of the angels. Hence, I was glad to find on Friday night (February 12th) a crowded gathering at the meeting which Mrs Philip Snowden so ably addressed at St John's Hall (Margate). Mrs Snowden, though a woman suffragist – and a good 'un – is not one of those flurried females who, in the course of their "raging and tearing propaganda" insult Cabinet Ministers, upset public meetings, and bring the blush of shame to the countenances of the London policemen, who bear them away from scenes of strife such as those witnessed at the Albert Hall not long since. Mrs Snowden is an orator; she gives reasons for the faith that is in her. I am no woman, but I confess that the speech of the lady whose husband is the Member for Blackburn has almost persuaded me to become a suffragette.[4]

Mrs Snowden said:

In the North of England, the supporters of women's franchise now outnumber the total electorate. Men make laws for women in total ignorance of what women themselves want. There is legislation pending even now which would materially injure the prospects of working women. After an unsuccessful bid to rid the barmaids of their employment, next summer Mr. Burns intends to introduce a Bill to stop ALL married women from working - and all this without even consulting them . . .

In reply to the old adage that women belonged at home Mrs Snowden added:

So is a man's place home. He ought to be there when spending his leisure time in the public house or club. . . if it were not for the women where would all the soldiers and sailors come from? If they wanted women to fight they are quite capable of fighting. Women beat men every time for endurance.

In answer to the Rev. Sir C.J.M. Shaw, she said that the suffragette agitation in England had given the impetus to similar movements in other countries and that American women were beginning to get indignant about their country's unclean politics. Further questioned, the speaker admitted she could not condemn the tactics of the militant suffragettes in their crusade against the Cabinet Minister. She said "women cannot express their opinions at the ballot box and must necessarily adopt some other method".

Following an unsuccessful attempt to see Mr Asquith, two suffragettes, Miss McLellan and Miss Solomon, failed in their attempt to post themselves as human letters to Downing Street from the East Strand Post Office!

In March 1909 Mrs Teresa Billington-Grieg, the first woman suffragist to be sent to Holloway Prison, came to speak to the Margate Pioneer Society. She defended the militant methods of the women suffragists but said "it was not correct to say that the Suffragists used hatpins (laughter); the hatpin existed only in the imagination of the penny-a-line reporter". She went on to say that: "Women were just as entitled to go in deputation to legislators as men were, and they were content to suffer a certain amount of temporary brutality in order to put a stop to injustice."

She felt that "People who condemned the militant methods of the suffragists must condemn every other fight for liberty . . . Women were outlawed from constitutional methods and had no alternative but to resort to violence" but that

1908-1909

A shop window display in 1912

this had been "of a much more modified type than that adopted by men in their struggles for political reform".[5]

Mrs Pember-Reeves, wife of the late Agent General of New Zealand, spoke at an NUWSS meeting in Ramsgate in March.. She spoke of enfranchisement in New Zealand, saying that she had now twice voted and that in New Zealand men now handed the newspaper to their wives first at the breakfast table. Miss Kennett, a head teacher from Ipswich, also spoke and responded to the anti-suffragist argument that women were incapable of thinking "imperially" by saying she did not quite understand what this meant but she did know that "some men thought in imperial pints on polling days (laughter)"[6]

At an NUWSS meeting in Thanet in April a large audience was told that the "Antis", were trying to make out that the suffragists were asking for many things which they did not, in fact, desire. Mrs Vickers asked if anyone could say what was most likely to take a woman away from her home "constantly attending meetings of local committees, or going to vote once every five years or so?"[7] This was probably a dig at Lady Rose Weigall, who was active in various public bodies in Thanet, and was also on the Anti-Suffrage League Committee.

> We have known a Member (MP) who had "no time" to receive a deputation of women suffragists from his own constituency, but who was known to spend many hours in entertaining the fair sex to tea on the terrace.[8]

A large NUWSS meeting in Thanet was addressed by Lady Francis Balfour. She said:

> As long as women are disqualified from voting, it is a stamp and a badge of inferiority. Why have women not got the vote? Why are they not treated as

Women in Kent

full citizens? Because all over the world in all nations – less perhaps in some than others – they have been considered inferior and classed in the eye of the law with more unfortunate people who are inferior – with paupers, lunatics, idiots and peers! (laughter) That is why we want the women to think on this subject.

Lady Balfour traced the history of the movement from the start. She referred to Mrs. Henry Fawcett, saying she had given 40 years of her life to the cause. She said the movement began with the question of the repeal of the Corn Law; then in 1867 J S Mill wrote his great book which had so much to do with women workers. Then came the Primrose League, which put men and women on an equal footing, then the Women's Liberal Association. She said the Liberal party owed a great deal to women. (The liberals were in power at the time.) In 1892 Prime Minister Balfour had stated that it was impossible for him to declare that women were unfitted to take their share in the constitution of the country. Many bills had been introduced by private members with the idea of giving women the vote. Lady Balfour said the militant suffragettes were only following those men who fought for the franchise in 1832 and 1867. She referred to those "well-to-do women who had never felt the pinch of care and want," and who said "why should we care about a vote?" These women, she said, "would not open their eyes and see the sufferings of their sisters".[9]

> *Lady Francis Balfour was the sister-in-law of Prime Minister Arthur Balfour. A noted biographer, she campaigned for the emancipation of women but disapproved of the militant activities of Emily Pankhurst. She was a capable orator and spoke out on issues of the day. Her biography of Dr Elsie Inglis was published in 1918.*

On 16th April 1909 a crowd of around a thousand supporters cheered Mrs Emmeline Pethwick-Lawrence as she left Holloway Prison after serving a two-month sentence.

In May 1909 a Grand Suffrage Bazaar or Exhibition was held in the Prince's Skating Rink in Knightsbridge.

Exhibits also included two replica prison cells! A banner around the walls read: "They that sow in tears shall reap in joy." Sales from all the handicraft stalls earned over £5,000 for the WSPU campaign fund.

At the end of June 1909 Marion Wallace Dunlop was arrested for stencilling a quotation from the 1689 Bill of Rights on the wall of St Stephen's Hall at the Palace of Westminster.

She became the first suffragette prisoner to refuse food in protest against her imprisonment in Holloway. Other suffragettes began to follow her example demanding to be treated as political prisoners, not common criminals. Shortly afterwards the force-feeding of prisoners began.

1908-1909
Open-Air Meetings

The organiser arrives in a town where she knows no one and has, at present, no idea of the amount of sympathy she is likely to meet with. She will first ascertain what, if any, local organisations go in for out-door meetings. (If there is a Labour or Socialist Party in the town it is pretty certain that open-air propaganda is done). – and at once approach the leaders of these organisations. She will probably find them most courteous and friendly, and from them she will learn what open spaces there are in the town where meetings can be held, what times and what days of the week are most suitable for such meetings, what likelihood there is of their being well attended, and she will gather a great deal more very valuable information by the way. For instance, they will tell her not only what she could learn at the Police Station – whether there is a by-law against chalking the flags but also whether such by-law, if it exists, is strictly enforced. They will also be able to suggest the best "pitches" for chalking and have even been known, where fully in sympathy with the cause, to lend a hand in the chalking! Information they will probably be able, also, to afford her, about various factories and works in the town – the numbers of men and women employed, their dinner-hour and time of leaving in the afternoon, and whether, outside, there are open spaces available for meetings.

More fruit, so far as the Branch is concerned, may be expected from the evening meetings, though in some ways they present far greater difficulties than those held in the dinner-hour. If chalking is forbidden, or the day is wet, the organiser really has no means of advertising. Distribution of leaflets to the passers-by with word of the meeting may cause a few to loiter, but, unless she has friends with her who will form a "decoy" group, she need not hope to have any listeners until she has been speaking for a few minutes. To ask those who linger perhaps on the other side of the Square, to come closer, is fatal: they will probably vanish altogether.

Well she must mount her chair and start – she is very unfortunate if she cannot shortly attract a few children, to whom a woman on a chair in the road is a novelty: and even a few grinning infants are better than nothing as a start. Not that they always show their interest in the most gratifying way. She may find herself the butt for dirty little caps, orange-peel, and various refuse, and the centre of a hideous concert of squeals, whistles, and shouts. However, this will probably be the signal for a few of the loiterers to wander up in nonchalant fashion, very loth to look as if they had any intention of listening, and then like a snowball the crowd gathers. "Nil desperandum" should surely be the motto of the open-air speaker. If she will only talk on, in faith, to space, the meeting will, like Topsy, grow.

This, of course, only touches the fringe of a big subject. Crowds are of many tempers: we have indicated only the good-natured and somewhat apathetic. However, it is matter of general experience that a hostile reception at first is often made up for by double enthusiasm later, so even a greeting of rotten eggs need prove no discouragement.[10]

Women in Kent

On the Sands, Margate

This postcard view of Margate beach, postmarked 29th July 1909, shows bathing machines, and deckchairs arranged for an entertainment or a meeting on the sands. There were often Christian beach missions or temperance crusades, but the suffragists also held meetings on the beach during the summer.

The suffragettes held several meetings in Broadstairs in July. Announcements were chalked on pavements all over the town. An open-air meeting was held in the Rose Inn Yard and a formal meeting of the Women's Freedom League was held on 13th July at the Pavilion in Broadstairs. Mrs. Holmes spoke of women's desire for liberty and self-government. They wanted the right to say under what conditions they should live and what laws they should obey, and what punishments should be inflicted on those who break the law. She said:

> It behoves every self-respecting woman to find out how her existence was considered a menace to the state. Why were women insulted with this mental and moral disqualification? Why should she be linked with lunatics and criminals? Women are justified in their existence, and perform the duties of citizenship. Women suffer in the Industrial world, and in the legal world, in a great many ways . . . women have suffered grievously from not having the vote. It is a political axiom that the interests of the unrepresented went to the wall . . . We are not pleading any privilege, but demand what we have a perfect right to have. (applause) Women have been asking for the vote for the last sixty years . . . because they behaved nicely and asked in a ladylike manner no attention was paid to them.

The life of working women in this country is little better than slavery . . . women in cities work 19 hours a day for a shilling a day.

1908-1909

Broadstairs bandstand in about 1910

She spoke of the plight of girls with unwanted pregnancies thus:

> Hundreds of girls who have committed a crime under the circumstances of mental and physical conditions only to be understood and grasped by women are tried by juries of men, the cases put by men and defended by men and judged by men. That girl could be sentenced to death or prison and they all knew there had been a partner in the crime who was morally as guilty as the girl, though the law cannot touch him. [The speaker was loudly applauded.][11]

> Mrs. Holmes from Croydon was on the National Executive Committee of the Women's Freedom League. She had been due to speak in Thanet earlier in the year but had to decline due to illness.

In August 1909 it was made illegal for women to attend public gatherings, especially those organized by the Liberal Party. Suffragettes therefore hung around outside such meetings making as much noise as they could. A few in Liverpool started to throw stones and were immediately arrested.

Alys Russell, a frequent contributor, wrote this very detailed and intimate account of an open-air meeting at Minster on the Isle of Sheppey in Kent for *The Common Cause*.

> We fixed on a grassy slope, by the beautiful old Abbey Gate House, for our meeting, always having National Union leaflets behind us. At seven o'clock a few ladies took the front seat on the grassy bank, while village children and country holiday children from London swarmed behind them.

Women in Kent

The picture shows the Abbey Church of SS Mary and Sexburga, Minster on the Isle of Sheppey.

The chair [sic!] was taken by Mr W A Jewson, a cliff cottage-holder of Eastchurch, who, as a member of the Men's League and the husband of a Suffragette, is an ardent supporter of our Cause. As he spoke, a crowd of about fifty gradually collected, mostly sailors or trippers from Sheerness, though Minster was also represented by the venerable clergyman and his daughter and others. After my address, which the noise and heat and dust rather curtailed, Miss Kate Raleigh, a prominent member of the Uxbridge National Society, gave an impressive and dignified answer to the physical force argument, and the meeting closed with questions, and a collection (in a child's sand-pail) of 2s 5d halfpenny. The audience listened most attentively, and we were delighted when some of them turned up at our Eastchurch meeting three evenings later. There we had a real "chair", an old landau lent by a friendly publican, and the audience of over 100 was, except for the clergyman and summer residents from Warden, composed almost entirely of labourers and their wives, who had come into Eastchurch for their Saturday's shopping. They listened for over an hour to our addresses, the only disturbance coming from an old man in a smock, Benjamin Bunk, who very evidently had already had his "arf-pint", and who, to our relief soon went off to get another one. I have seldom addressed such a perfectly serious audience – one very roughly dressed young labourer standing immovable and rapt the whole time, only relaxing at the end to drop several coppers in our pail. Mr Jewson got a very good show of hands for our resolution, and Miss Raleigh undertook to help to form a local society of the National Union, and to start their funds with our two collections. I have had to leave Sheppey, but Miss Raleigh, from her summer cottage there, and with the help of Mr and Mrs Jewson, will carry on the work among these friendly and intelligent island dwellers.[12]

A letter from Miss Cicely Hamilton, author of *Marriage as a Trade* to one of the daily papers was reprinted in the *Thanet Times*. An ardent suffragette, she says that:

... anyone really conversant with the movement would have discovered that the suffragist is out for a good deal more than just the vote. That is merely the outward sign of a desire for something considerably more important. It is merely one of the inevitable results of the greatest discovery of the age: the

1908-1909

discovery by women of their own identity . . . the real work of the suffragist is not the gaining of votes; it is the production of women that want them. [13]

> Cicely Hamilton had joined the WSPU in 1908 but disliked the autocratic way in which Mrs Pankhurst ran the organisation so she left to join the Women's Freedom League. She was also a founder member of the Actresses' and the Women Writers' Suffrage Leagues. Cicely Hamilton wrote two propaganda plays about suffrage, How the Vote was Won (1909) and A Pageant of Great Women. Perhaps her most important contribution to the feminist movement was her influential book, Marriage as a Trade, published in 1909. Cicely Hamilton argued that woman were brought up to look for success only in the marriage market, and this severely damaged their intellectual development.

In October 1909 over one hundred doctors, among them Dr Forbes Winslow and the surgeon Mansell-Moullin, signed a letter to the Prime Minister Asquith protesting about the forced feeding of suffragist prisoners and outlining the risks.

At a WSPU meeting in the Empress Rooms in Cliftonville: "In weather that would give pause to the bravest of mere men, lady advocates of votes for women assembled in good numbers last night to hear a debate on the all-engrossing topic." The champion of the suffragists was Miss Helen Ogston, of the WSPU and the opposite viewpoint in the controversy was stated by Dr Douglas Cockburn representing the Men's League for Opposing Women Suffrage.

Dr Cockburn spoke first then Miss Ogston replied that:

> The politics of today concerned the home and women's sphere. The State over-rode individual liberty and decided the every-day questions in which women's specialised knowledge was necessary – questions such as housing, the children and their education, temperance, and so on. The concession of the vote to women was a necessity and a right. . . . Women had all the penalties and pains of citizenship, and they rightly demanded a voice in the management of the nation's affairs. Women were told that they should remain outside the turmoil of politics, but men were glad enough that they should do the canvassing and the other dirty work of politics. They had been used by men for their own ends and were quite willing to stay in politics a little longer for theirs.

The report concluded that:

> Miss Ogston went on in detail to make mincemeat of the arguments of the other side. A resolution that the Parliamentary vote ought to be given to women on the same terms as it is, or may be, given to men, was then carried by 60 votes to 22.[14]

The reporter hoped to give a full report of the debate in the next issue – "floods permitting"!

Women in Kent

> *Helen Ogston had gained some publicity on 5th December 1908 when as one of a large group of hecklers at the Royal Albert Hall she wielded a dog-whip to fend off the stewards who were trying to evict her from the hall. Lloyd George, then Liberal Chancellor the Exchequer, and well-known for his anti-suffrage views, took two hours to complete his speech claiming "I have no desire to speak by gracious permission of Queen Christabel."*

On 10th November 1909, Mrs Charlotte Despard of the Women's Freedom League gave an eloquent speech at Margate. The Chairman announced that the society had been formed in Thanet to embrace both the militant and non-militant sections of the women's movement. He thought it disgraceful that anti-suffrage women were running down the suffragists who were fighting for women's rights. Rev. G Hinscliff spoke for the suffrage. Mrs Despard said the movement was getting stronger and stronger, and that some of the best men were with them. She said that the cause was not anti-men; the Women's Freedom League to which she belonged was helping to make women equal with men and bring about women's economic freedom. Her speech ended with loud applause.

Jessie Kenney, sister of Annie, tried to gain admittance to an audience with Mr Asquith disguised as a telegraph boy!

The Common Cause published a report of a meeting in the Congregational Hall in Ramsgate where: "It was satisfactory to see that the male section of the audience was much larger than at former meetings. The hall was decorated with NU posters, a good deal of literature was sold, and a collection taken at the door." Members were despondent that:

> There seems no hope of either candidate proclaiming himself in favour of women's suffrage. It is anticipated that a deputation of electors will shortly wait on Mr Norman Craig, the unionist candidate, to lay before him women's claims; but electors here are very slow in coming forward with help. Workers are badly needed before the voters' petition can be started.[15]

For Christmas 1909 *Votes for Women* was advertising "a highly artistic table game" called Pank-a-Squith! It cost 1/6d at all WSPU shops and was based on the attempt of suffragettes to get from their homes to the Houses of Parliament. They had to cross fifty sections and met with all sorts of obstacles en route. The game was printed in the Union colours of purple, white and green.

The election policy of the NUWSS at the end of 1909 was: "to help no candidate unless they declare themselves to be supporters of votes for women, and pledge to oppose extending the franchise to all adult men if this does not include women".[16]

1908-1909

This charming tailor-made was advertised in the Thanet Times *throughout March 1909.*

---

[1] TT 4th November 1908
[2] DT February 1909
[3] TT 17th February 1909
[4] Ibid
[5] TT 31st March 1909
[6] TT 7th April 1909
[7] Ibid
[8] CC 22nd April 1909
[9] TT 28th April 1909
[10] CC 3rd June 1909
[11] TT 14th July 1909
[12] CC 19th August 1909
[13] TT 22nd September 1909
[14] TT 29th October 1909
[15] CC December 16th 1909
[16] TT 15th December 1909

Chapter Seven

1910

There are thousands of women in this movement ready to lay down their lives for the cause. (Mrs Pethick Lawrence writing in *Votes for Women*, 13th October 1909)

The NUWSS opened a committee room at 5 King Street in Ramsgate in January 1910, during the General Election campaign. In most of the local newspapers in Kent it was tariff reform and the price of hops which were important questions at this time, not female suffrage. Some women, however, were determined to dress appropriately for the occasion.

Velvet or votes

As the important period of the General Election is quickly approaching, our women, anxious to help and work for their friends, for their country, are busy ordering costumes for the campaign. . . velvet is the prevailing note in these charming creations, which seem ideal gowns for the occasion. [1]

Under the headline "Voteless yet vote getters" this report shows that women were playing an active part in the election campaign.

Ladies are also rendering splendid service . . . A novelty in electioneering in Thanet is the activity of the members of the fair sex in the role of hecklers, and it is noteworthy that the questions put by the ladies are always pointed and clever, as well as disconcerting the speakers.[2]

Frank Fagg, a Canterbury grocer used this clever slogan for the first few months of the year. "Every woman votes for our reliable margarine."[3]

Mrs Pankhurst called a truce on all militant acts by the WSPU while the committee drafted the Conciliation Committee Women's Franchise Bill. Although this Bill would only offer voting rights to property-owning women it was seen as very small step in the right direction if it could gain parliamentary support.

This extract is from a poem attributed to Lancelot Cayley Shadwell that appeared in the *East Kent Times* in January 1910.

A Political ABC
S are the suffragettes, keen and alert
To badger poor Ministers, giving them jumps
When going to jail they are cheeky and pert
But they soon simmer down if you say "Stomach pumps."[4]

Towards the end of January Haley's Comet was visible in the Canterbury area. All those looking at this "luminous stranger" had "an excellent view."[5]

In February 1910 the Liberals won the General Election.

> *In a Punch cartoon of 9th February 1910 a benevolent old gentleman has just given a penny to Miss A of Park Lane, who is selling Votes for Women. He insists that he doesn't want a copy of the newspaper. "No, no, keep the paper, my good woman, keep the paper!"*

> This week has been taken up with preparations for Mrs Pankhurst's meetings, including an evening gathering kindly arranged by Mrs Berry in Margate, an open-air meeting on the sands at Margate, two open-air meetings at Hodgman's yard in Ramsgate, an At Home at Broadstairs and a drawing room meeting at St Martin's in Margate hosted by Miss Courtenay-Page.[6]

Mrs Emmeline Pankhurst, leader of the WSPU addressed a meeting in Ramsgate on Thursday 21st April 1910.

> Those expecting to behold a massive hooligan will be agreeably surprised at the dainty appearance of the refined and cultured women who will appeal to them with her moving account of the sad conditions under which unrepresented women-workers are struggling for a livelihood.[7]

"A charming little procession of dog-carts, decorated in the union colours" was to advertise Mrs Pankhurst's meeting in the streets of Canterbury.[8]

On 22nd April Mrs Pankhurst spoke to over 400 people at St Margaret's Hall in Canterbury. She stated that "over four hundred members of the House of Commons had given a very businesslike pledge in favour of Woman's Suffrage". At the end, she was asked if a woman would be breaking her marriage vows if she did not vote as her husband wished. Amused, she replied that "a woman does take a vow about obeying her husband, and I suppose it holds just as good as the promise a man makes to endow his wife with all his worldly goods".[9]

Mrs Pankhurst's pending visit to Thanet was advertised by "a coach and four. Miss Macaulay, the local organiser for Canterbury and Thanet, was seated on the box, and the coach was gaily decorated with the colours of the militant

1910

During the 1910 General Election campaign in Canterbury

This photo, taken outside the Royal Victoria Pavilion in Ramsgate, appeared in Votes For Women *in April 1910. It is reproduced here courtesy of the Women's Library*

Other women had been advertising their leader's visit with a more hands-on approach. "Suffragettes have been making some of the public walls in Ramsgate hideous with their announcements written in chalk."[11]

A week later they were thanked by name in the weekly branch report in *Votes for Women*.

"Mrs Pankhurst's visit is over but the splendid meetings she addressed will not soon be forgotten here, and an excellent foundation for future work has been laid". Mrs Brewster, Miss Dyer, and the Misses Simmons were thanked for chalking.[12]

These "Snapshots" appeared in the *East Kent Times* at the end of April:-

Mrs Pankhurst says that every stone thrown by a suffragette has been carefully chosen.

Among the articles which can be purchased from the militant WSPU in the society's colours we notice the significant item – hat pins at 6d, 9d, and 1s.[13]

Mrs Pankhurst spoke at the WSPU meeting in the Royal Victoria Pavilion in Ramsgate. She was described as "a woman of remarkable personal magnetism and a brilliant convincing speaker, although physically not a strong woman".

Her visit to Ramsgate was:

hugely placarded, for days beforehand a coach was driven about the town blazoning forth the colours of the propagandists, and exhibiting notices of the meeting, and on Thursday in last week, the day of the meeting at the Pavilion Theatre, townspeople awoke to find the pavements and promenades covered with cheap advertisements in chalk.

Mrs Pankhurst spoke to an almost full auditorium about the extraordinary growth of the women's suffrage movement which was due she felt to the fact that its advocates had met with opposition: "No one ever thought of opposing a new movement unless headway was being made. Apathy and indifference had been their biggest obstacles, but these were now fast disappearing." She ended by saying: "If you have courage enough, if you are persistent, you are bound to win in the end if only your cause, like ours, is right."[14]

The following day Mrs Pankhurst spoke at the Theatre Royal in Margate (*right* circa 1903). Some young men heckled her at the beginning of the meeting but withdrew when the speaker hurled seething remarks at them. Mrs Pankhurst claimed that women who paid rates, taxes and rent, or held a university degree should have a vote on equal terms with men. She urged the women of Thanet to support the women's franchise, and added that although the militant party to which she belonged had stayed their hand for the present there would be more drastic measures taken to keep their cause before the public unless their reasonable demands were conceded. According to statistics quoted in a letter to the paper on 26th March 1910, that would mean that about a million and a quarter women would then possess the vote in addition to the seven-and-a-half million men.[15]

The Ramsgate branch of the NUWSS held a successful cake sale at 8 Royal Crescent on Wednesday 20th April at the home of Margaret Sale, the Honorary Secretary. "They hope to have a large garden meeting in the summer months. The visit of Mrs Pankhurst to Ramsgate has done a great deal to rouse interest in the cause."[16]

The death of King Edward VII in May 1910 meant that reports of Mrs Pankhurst's meetings in Thanet were not printed in the *East Kent Times*.

In June the new Thanet headquarters of the WSPU was opened by Florence Macaulay at No 2 York Terrace, opposite Ramsgate Harbour. Members of the audience were urged to join in the Suffrage demonstration. which owing to the death of the King in May, had been postponed until Saturday 18th June.[17]

After tea a photograph of the group was taken by a member, Miss Gilmour Steill of Broadstairs. If only we could see that photograph now!

The suffrage procession in London

Florence Macaulay also wrote to the *Folkestone Herald* about the WSPU march in London:

> Special features of this splendid demonstration, the greatest that has ever been known, are the 480 white-clad prisoners; the white-haired pioneers of this

1910

movement; the great array of women graduates in cap and gown; the forty bands and the magnificent banners carried by all the processionists!

All women of Kent and Kentish women will be heartily welcomed under the "Invicta" banner, with its beautiful lighthouse, the work of a Ramsgate member of the WSPU, which will be found in Section B of the procession forming up close to Whitehall stairs.

Mr Baldwin, the excursion agent, is running a cheap day train on that date. 4s return from Thanet stations. 4s 6d returning Sunday.[18]

Votes for Women names the woman responsible for the banner as Miss M Wilson of Ramsgate.[19]

The suffragette procession held in London on 18th June 1910 was nearly two miles long. More than 10,000 people marched from the Embankment to the Royal Albert Hall accompanied by many bands. Some women were carrying flowers. £5,000 was raised for the WSPU campaign.

In July 1910 the independent Thanet Women's Suffrage Society was dissolved so that members could join the Canterbury and Thanet WSPU.

This photograph of the WSPU shop appeared in Votes for Women *in September 1910. It is reproduced here courtesy of the Women's Library.*

Christabel's visit

Christabel Pankhurst spoke to a large afternoon meeting at the Town Hall in Herne Bay on Friday 1st July. That evening she addressed a large crowd at the Royal Victoria Pavilion in Ramsgate.

> The purple, green and white colours of the WSPU were prominent in the hall, and the banner of the Canterbury and Thanet Branch stood upon the platform, together with a banner bearing the inspiring message "Spur thee to thy goal".
>
> Miss Pankhurst spoke for considerably more than an hour. She told the tale of "a man who lost his latch-key and broke a window to get into his own house". The British constitution, she said was women's house. They had been robbed of their latch-key and they were going to break the window to get in (loud applause).

The reporter adds that:

> There is nothing of the "blue stocking" of popular conception in the appearance of Miss Pankhurst – her charm of manner, the frank, open face and winning smile, together with the determined mouth and chin, the expressive eyes and brilliant ability, make in Miss Pankhurst the ideal leader of the cause which she so valiantly champions.[20]

At the Herne Bay meeting the chairman of the Urban District Council, Mr H E Ramsay JP presided. He claimed to have been advocating woman's suffrage for the last twenty years and felt that "sex disability should be eternally wiped out".[21]

Christabel spoke at the Theatre Royal in Margate on Saturday 2nd July. After the meeting members were invited to a "Family Party" at the home of Mrs Barnett-Smith in Cliftonville Avenue so that they could meet Christabel.

Suffragettes posing for a group photograph outside the Theatre Royal in 1910 which appeared in the East Kent Times of 6th July 1910. Christabel Pankhurst is in the centre of the group holding the spray of flowers. The photographer was Mr G Houghton of Margate. (Reproduced here by kind permission of Richard Clements.)

1910

Also reported in the *East Kent Times* under the heading "How to suppress suffragists" is one man's solution to the woman suffrage problem!:

> Speaking at the crowning of the Rose Queen at Lytham a Mr Wykeham Clifton ventured to remark that if the suffragists had been treated with the cat-o-nine-tails their agitation would have been ended long ago!![22]

A letter to the Editor from "A Canterbury Woman Suffragist" reminded supporters of the cause to write to Kent MPs in support of the second reading of the Woman Suffrage Bill due on either 11th or 12th July. She added that the Canterbury MP Henniker Heaton was a strong supporter of the Bill, and that a large demonstration would be held in London on 23rd July, in support of "Votes for Women". She ends her letter with these words: "The suffrage cause is at a critical stage in its fortunes, a long pull, a strong pull, a pull altogether – and victory is assured."[23]

On 12th July 1910 the Women's Suffrage Bill passed its second reading in the House of Commons with a majority of 109 even though the Prime Minister, Mr Asquith, and the Chancellor, Lloyd George, voted against it.

In *The Common Cause* they were yet again asking for help in selling the paper during the summer holidays.

> We are glad to report that the splendid arrangements made for selling the paper in Trafalgar Square on the 9th resulted in nearly 1,400 being sold. A large number was also sold at the Anti-Suffrage demonstration on the 16th, and we wish to thank most heartily those friends who gave up their precious Saturday afternoons to this useful form of propaganda. More than ever in the history of the movement is it vital that the aims and policy of the National Union should be well known and clearly understood, and it is for us to keep alive by every means in our power the intense, universal interest shown in the question of the enfranchisement of women. During the holiday weeks when meetings are few the best way of working for our cause is by helping to sell *The Common Cause*, getting new subscribers, selling at seaside places, leaving the paper at seaside reading-rooms, in hotels, waiting-rooms, on piers, inducing newsagents to stock the paper and show our weekly poster, and so on. The manager will be delighted to receive suggestions, or to send supplies of this paper, and will be grateful to those who send word of difficulty in obtaining the paper, so that the difficulty may be promptly removed.[24]

On 23rd July 1910 another successful rally was held in Hyde Park.

> Votes for Women published some "Hints for the Procession".
> DON'T
> Don't wear gowns that have to be held up
> Don't wear enormous hats that block the view
> Don't wave handkerchiefs
> DO
> Wear white if possible[25]

Women in Kent

York Terrace in Ramsgate in about 1910. The WSPU shop is the building on the right with a balcony

On 24th July 1910 Asquith announced that the Conciliation Bill will be given no more time in the current Parliamentary session.

Speaking at a Primrose League gathering at Ramsgate in July Mr Norman Craig KC, MP for Thanet, admitted that his views on the subject of votes for women had somewhat changed, and he recognised that it was his duty in the circumstances either to justify or fail to justify his position:

> Vast numbers of women were now isolated and working as commercial as well as social units. Of woman it could no longer be said that she was merely the complement of man, actually and domestically. Consequent upon the change which had come about he did think the time had now arrived when women should be granted representation in the legislature.[26]

The following week it was reported that the WSPU flag that Miss Gertrude Harraden had been flying from a flagstaff in front of her bungalow in Walmer "had been cut down by some person or persons unknown, and much indignation and sympathy have been aroused in the neighbourhood".[27]

The WSPU urged any suffragist visitors to East Kent to visit their office in Ramsgate where they could purchase "a large and varied choice of literature, badges, stationery etc.in the colours" as well as items from the "Pound Stall" where tea, cocoa, jam etc. could be purchased "as well as Miss Rosa Lightman's lavender preparations".[28]

At the end of August women in Canterbury were offered this advice on "Wife-made men".

> We hear much about self-made men. It might do us good to hear more about wife-made men. There are a lot of them. Many of the best men in the world – the greatest in statesmanship, science, art and literature – have freely

1910

acknowledged their indebtedness to women. Perhaps they are indebted to their wives, perhaps to other women. A wise wife is she who is a comrade and a source of inspiration. If she is not a comrade some other woman may be. Not every wife earnestly seeks to be a helpful companion. Not everyone who tries succeeds. The wife who contributes to her husband's uplift and helps to enlarge his vision must not be denied high credit for his career. The best part of any man is the femininity which comes from his wife. The high character which counts for his success may have originated from her; to her he may owe his purposes. And her joy in it is exquisite. It is the women's greatest work.[29]

Open-air meetings were still being held in September. "At Walmer and Dover, Mrs Arnett, a sweated worker, received a most sympathetic hearing from rich and poor alike for her graphic first-hand description of the lives of so many women workers."[30]

Mrs Pethick-Lawrence was also in East Kent on several occasions in 1910. She spoke at Folkestone Town Hall in July, then at Herne Bay Town Hall on 21st September. The next day she and her husband visited the new WSPU office in Ramsgate overlooking the harbour. It had been fitted up almost entirely by generous gifts from members and their friends.[31] Mrs Pethick-Lawrence was booked to speak at the Theatre Royal in Margate on 11th November.

Folkestone Town Hall, now a bookshop, seen here before porch added

On 13th October 1910 Christabel Pankhurst spoke at a WSPU meeting at Folkestone Town Hall. This was on the fifth anniversary of her violent rejection from the Free Trade Hall in Manchester. A number of questions were handed to Miss Pankhurst on pieces of paper at the end of the meeting. Here are her answers to some of them:

> Do you not think your tactics have alienated numbers of people who were friendly to your cause?
>
> No I do not. They might have alienated some people who pretended to be friendly but really were not. We are glad to be rid of such friends as that.

Women in Kent

Won't the Conciliation Bill enfranchise mostly Conservative women? Mr Lloyd George as good as said so.

He has no facts whatsoever to support his statement. The Bill will enfranchise women of all shades of political opinion.

There are so many more women than men in the country that if women had the vote would not the country be governed more by women than men?

That is a mistake as regards the Conciliation Bill. There are only about one-sixth as many women householders as men. The total number of women in the country, moreover, is only slightly more than the number of men.[32]

The first committee meeting of the Kentish Federation of the NUWSS was held in Tonbridge on 5th October 1910. Delegates attended from Tunbridge Wells, Tonbridge, Sevenoaks, Folkestone, Ramsgate and Dover. Miss Taylor of Tonbridge kindly consented to act as Honorary Secretary and the committee hoped that Miss Lucy Deane, president of the Sevenoaks Society, would consider becoming chairman.

Those of her audience who will hear Mrs Pankhurst for the first time on Wednesday night, will probably be expecting to see a "formidable looking hooligan," claims an anonymous follower writing in the *Dover Express*. The founder of the WSPU was, however, "a slight, fragile altogether charming woman, who in addition to the right word, the happy gesture, the low, sweet

Mrs Emmeline Pankhurst was due to speak at Dover Town Hall on 26th October 1910. This photograph from the Dover Express *shows women in cars hired to drive them round the town to advertise the meeting.*[33] *I apologise for the rather poor quality of the original but as this was one of the first photographs I found of suffragists in any local newspaper I thought it should be included.*

1910

VOTES FOR WOMEN
Women's Social and Political Union.
(PURPLE, WHITE, & GREEN).

A MEETING will be held in the
**DOVER TOWN HALL,
WEDNESDAY, OCT. 26th,**
At 8 p.m. SPEAKER:
Mrs. PANKHURST
"Political Emancipation must precede Social Regeneration."
Tickets 2s. 6d., 1s.; 6d., of Wm. Dawson & Son, Ltd:
Early Door for Ticket holders only, under the clock.

This advertisement appeared in the Dover Express.[34]

voice, possesses also that wonderful magnetic personality peculiar to the born leader". The writer considered it "a strange and pitiful thing that her country could find no better reward for such genius and devotion than the broad arrow and the criminal's cell".[35]

Friday 10th November 1910 came to be known as "Black Friday". The Conciliation Bill had been delayed by the dissolution of Parliament. Mrs Pankhurst declared that the truce, which had been in force since the General Election, was now over, so 300 delegates of the WSPU marched from Caxton Hall to the House of Commons. In Parliament Square the police subjected them to levels of brutality not before encountered.

A letter from Mr C Mansell-Moullin, Vice-President of the Royal College of Surgeons to the *Daily Mail* describes the scene:

Women in Kent

> The women were treated with the greatest brutality. They were pushed about in all directions and thrown down by the police. Their arms were twisted until they were almost broken. Their thumbs were forcibly bent back, and they were tortured in other nameless ways that made one feel sick at the sight.

The writer was also convinced that "bands of roughs" had been employed by the police to charge into the groups of women, "throwing the women down, and trampling upon them". His wife was a suffragette, and he later also spoke out against force-feeding of prisoners.[36]

On Friday 11th November 1910 Mrs Pethwick-Lawrence spoke to a WSPU meeting in the Theatre Royal in Margate.

The *Dover Express* published a letter from the Conservative and Unionist Women's Franchise Association, addressed to all those MPs who had voted in favour of the second reading of the Conciliation Bill.

> The House of Commons has done us the honour to declare frequently, by large majorities, that women ought to have the vote, though it seems to find some difficulty in translating this conviction into an Act. It seems to us that it has been proved that women of the Anglo-Saxon race use political power quite as wisely as men. Queens have ruled, both absolutely and constitutionally, with a large measure of success. In local government, women, whether as members of local bodies or voters, have shown themselves no whit less sensible than their husbands and brothers. Therefore, it is reasonable to suppose they would use the Parliamentary vote well if they were entrusted with it. There is another reason which makes it especially desirable that women should have a voice in politics at the present time. Parliament is showing an increasing disposition to undertake social legislation. Laws are being projected and passed regulating our schools, the relations of parents to children, the housing of the working classes, the conditions under which midwives may practise or women workers earn their living, even the age at which we may allow our sons to smoke, and the kind of fender we must put up in our kitchens when we have young children. We really think our opinion would be very useful on all these matters, to say nothing of such serious questions as the alteration of the divorce law, and we certainly feel we should have a voice in deciding what men are to make the laws under which we have to live, since many of these primarily affect us. That is all we ask for.[37]

A *Punch* cartoon from 30th November 1910 showed a suffragette protest in the background. There were lots of banners and posters being waved but otherwise the people are shown realistically.

Bobby & Co Ltd of Margate were offering this delightful hat to the readers of the Thanet Times on 1st April 1910.

[1] EKT 5th January 1910
[2] TT 14th January 1910
[3] KGCP 15th January 1910
[4] EKT 19th January 1910
[5] KGCP 29th January 1910
[6] VW 22nd April 1910
[7] EKT 23rd February 1910
[8] VW 8th April 1910
[9] KGCP 23rd April 1910
[10] EKT 20th April 1910
[11] TT 23rd April 1910
[12] VW 29th April 1910
[13] EKT 26th April 1910
[14] TT 29th April 1910
[15] TT 26th March 1910
[16] CC 5th May 1910
[17] EKT 1st June 1910
[18] EKT 8th June 1910
[19] VW 11th June 1910
[20] EKT 6th July 1910
[21] KGCP 9th July 1910
[22] EKT 6th July 1910
[23] KGCP 9th July 1910
[24] CC 21st July 1910
[25] VW 22nd July 1910
[26] TT 29th July 1910
[27] VW 12th August 1910

[28] VW 19th August 1910
[29] KGCP 27th August 1910
[30] VW 16th September 1910
[31] VW 30th September 1910
[32] FH 15th October 1910
[33] DE 28th October 1910
[34] DE 21st October 1910
[35] DE 21st October 1910
[36] Daily Mail 22nd November 1910
[37] DE 11th November 1910

Chapter Eight

1911 and 1912

The Split
Two ladies sitting opposite each other in a restaurant. Budding suffragette: "I say Prissy (with intensity) Are you a Peth or a Pank?" (*Punch* cartoon, 30th October 1912)

1911

The Parliamentary Franchise (Women's) Bill, which would give votes to women householders, was due for a second reading in Parliament in May. The Women's procession in London was postponed from May to June because of King George V's coronation. Suffragettes began smashing windows in London's West End when the government changed tactics over the Suffrage Bill.

In Dover two issues concerning the townsfolk that year were whether or not to allow trams on Sunday, and whether they should have a free library.

At the meeting of the Royal Drawing Society in the Art Gallery of the Guildhall, on January 13th the gold star for figure painting in oils was awarded to Miss Agnes Shelley Horsley for a life-sized portrait of herself. Miss Horsley is a keen suffragist and is WSPU literature secretary in Canterbury. The presentation was made by the Lord Mayor, who was accompanied by the Lady Mayoress.[1]

In February 1911, the *Kentish Gazette & Canterbury Press* published two readers' letters that suggested that there had been some confusion at the recent Anti-Suffrage meeting in Canterbury when it was declared that a resolution had been passed when "no invitation was given to those unfavourable to the resolution to express their opinion, in the usual way, by a show of hands".[2]

On 17th February Lady Brassey presided over an NUWSS meeting at Dover Town Hall. The speakers included Dr Flora Murray and the Reverend Hugh Chapman of the Chapel Royal of the Savoy in London. At this meeting Lady Brassey apologised for her husband, the Lord Warden's, absence but she felt it better he should stay away until he had made up his mind about their cause.[3] By the end of May 1911 Lord Brassey had come "off the fence", down on the side of women's suffrage and promised to support strongly the Conciliation Bill.[4]

A well attended NUWSS meeting held on 20th February in the Congregational Hall in Ramsgate was addressed by Mrs Rackham, a member of the Cambridge Poor Law Guardians.

Mrs M J Poole who presided said that the Thanet branch should make themselves "a very great power in the island and should exercise a benign influence so that they might by every means in their power advance the interests of the cause".

Mrs Rackham explained that the election policy of the NUWSS was to try and secure the return to Parliament of MPs who were in favour of the cause, quite irrespective of party. This policy had been successful as 408 out of 670 MPs were now in favour of women's suffrage. She hoped they could convert the remaining 193 "dark horses" too.[5]

Mr Ronald Freeley, a Dover councillor, joked at a meeting about Sunday trams which was causing strong feeling in the town. He had recently described Dover as "in a hobble skirt" but now he felt she was wearing a "harem skirt" as she was "a little divided".[6]

Mrs Pethick-Lawrence spoke at a meeting in the Foresters' Hall in Canterbury on Thursday 17th March 1911. The other speaker was Mr Duval from the Men's Union in favour of Women's Suffrage. Mrs Pethick-Lawrence told her audience that women wanted the vote because "no class, no sex, no section of the community could win attention for its needs, or redress of its grievances unless that class, or sex or section was represented in the legislature". This remark brought loud applause.[7]

St Peter's Street in Canterbury in about 1911

Mrs M Renton from the NUWSS visited the Kent Federation in April 1911. She spent sixteen days in Kent and during this time she addressed meetings at Hildenborough, Tonbridge, Sevenoaks, Leigh and Ashford, where a new society was being set up. She also spent two days in Canterbury but "found work rather difficult there".[8]

A fresh Woman Suffrage Bill giving votes to woman householders was due for a second reading in Parliament on 9th May 1911. Dover Town Council passed a resolution approving this Bill as did "Manchester, Glasgow, Dublin. Dundee and about 35 other towns".[9] The only speaker opposed to it was Alderman Lewis, who claimed that the municipal vote should also "be withheld from about half the men ratepayers of Dover who habitually neglect to use it".[10]

1911 and 1912

Miss Florence Macaulay, organiser of the Canterbury and South Kent WSPU, wrote to local papers to remind women about the forthcoming procession in London to be held on Saturday 17th June. It had originally been planned for May 28th but had been postponed because of the King's coronation. It would be led by "General" Flora Drummond on horseback and, leaving Embankment at 5.30pm, would march via Trafalgar Square and Piccadilly to the Albert Hall, Kensington Town Hall and the Empress Rooms where meetings would be held. Speakers would include Mrs Pankhurst, Mrs Pethick-Lawrence, Miss Vida Goldstein and Miss Christabel Pankhurst. "It will consist of 5 miles of women walking seven abreast, carrying a thousand banners and supported by seventy bands." Their contingent would be "right at the front in Section A3, just behind the prisoners' pageant".[11] A special excursion train would leave Canterbury at 9.15am and leave for home from Charing Cross at just past midnight.

> Contingents from Margate, Ramsgate and Broadstairs will board the 8.58 train to London tomorrow to join the Women's Suffrage demonstration in London. The procession will be four miles long and will stretch from the Houses of Parliament to the Bank of England.
>
> There will be the purple, white and green of the WSPU, the red, white and green of the NUWSS, the green, white and gold of the Women's Freedom League, the beautiful colours of the Actresses Franchise League, of the Writers and Artists and all the numberless other special contingents. There will be a historical pageant of women representing notable characters from the dawn of history in our country down the present day. There will also be a special pageant of prisoners which will consist of over 700 women representing the number of imprisonments suffered by women since the militant movement began. Graduates will walk in their robes.[12]

Dr Annie Brunyate from Dover mentioned in a letter to the local paper that horse brakes would be provided for those who could not walk for too long. Seats on the brakes would cost one shilling each.

> Practical hints for processionists
>
> Wear the colours (red, white and green) conspicuously
>
> Be punctual. Arrive Whitehall 5pm
>
> Look for your number and banner
>
> Line up seven abreast
>
> Remain in your line once you have found it
>
> Keep step with the person on your left
>
> Keep a good line in marching
>
> Wheel carefully (when turning corners the inner man (sic!) should mark time while the outer men (sic!) are wheeling)
>
> Hold your head up and square your shoulders and remember you are part of a great demonstration
>
> When halts are called keep your ranks and stand at attention
>
> Do not look back or talk to the people behind you
>
> Leave a good space before and behind each banner
>
> Keep a uniform distance from the line in front

Women in Kent

After a halt to allow the passage of traffic don't attempt to catch up the people in front

Learn the words and music of the March and join heartily in singing it

Wear white if you can

Let your dress be short and your hat small

Bring a little food with you to eat while waiting[13]

The official programme lists all the societies and groups hoping to take part. These included the Women's Tax Resistance League, the Fabian Women's Group, the Women Sanitary Inspectors and Health Visitors, and a number of men's groups sympathetic to women's suffrage.

The accompanying letter urged all women to "LEAD ON!" and quoted this verse from Olive Schreiner:

> And Reason, that old man, said to her, "Silence, what do you hear?"
> And she listened intently and she said, "I hear the sound of feet, a thousand times ten
> Thousand and thousands of thousands, and they beat this way!"
> He said," They are the feet of those who shall follow you. Lead on!"

Olive Schreiner was a South African who originally came to England to study medicine at Elizabeth Garrett Anderson's medical school. She was involved in the suffrage movement and wrote a book, Women and Labour, in 1911. She was a pacifist and opposed the Boer Wars in South Africa in 1899. She returned to England in 1914 and was active in the peace movement throughout the First World War.

One paragraph urges the "Woman of Today – you whose instinct is to shrink from public action of any kind, will you be in those ranks on that day?" and ended by saying:

> This day when the women of the world's greatest city went forth in the might of their multitudes to demonstrate their love of liberty- the love that has made and kept Britain great – will be remembered in history. **Do not miss the honour and the privilege of taking your part.**

A *Daily Mail* reporter had written "I am sure a great many people never realised until yesterday how many young and dainty and elegant and charming most leaders of the movement are."

The *Kentish Gazette & Canterbury Press* reported that "Kent was represented by about five hundred women" and that there was a large contingent of "working women in poor circumstances" of which "many were Lancashire and Midland factory operators who had travelled down in the night, after working in the mills the previous day". Kentish members of the WSPU "marched under a magnificent banner bearing the White Horse of Kent on a blue ground". Lady Brassey, wife of the Lord Warden of the Cinque Ports, also marched with the Kent contingent.[14]

> The suffrage unions of Dover and Folkestone joined forces and walked together under one banner. This emblem had been designed and executed for the occasion by members of the Folkestone Society, in red, white and green, the colours of the National Union. Upon a shield of white were drawn the arms of

1911 and 1912

the two ports in red and green , and above them the names of the towns boldly printed in red. Beneath the crests was displayed in green the following stirring motto, adapted from the closing lines of Wordsworth's "Ode to the Men of Kent."

> No parleying now. In Britain is one breath.
> We are all with you now from shore to shore.
> Women of Kent, 'tis victory or death.

In the bottom corner of the banner were entwined the initial letters of Dover and Folkestone, in a wreath of red and green.[15]

This view of the procession is from a postcard held by Dover Discovery Centre.

Vida Goldstein and Muriel Matters, the Australian suffragists who had spoken at several meetings in Kent, marched proudly at the head of the Australia and New Zealand contingent which carried a banner proclaiming: "Trust the Women Mother as I have done." This banner was purchased back from the Fawcett Library in London in 1988 and in 2002 was donated to the Parliament House Gift Collection for permanent display to celebrate the centenary of the pioneering Commonwealth Franchise Act 1902, which granted most Australian women the right to vote and to stand for election to parliament.

The spectacle brought the area around Hyde Park Corner and Piccadilly to a standstill. Motor omnibuses were crowded with people who stood on the seats and cheered and shouted while they were stuck in the traffic. The people at the end of the procession were still marching at 8.30pm and could not get to the Albert Hall to hear the speeches. It was 10pm before the traffic started to flow normally again.

Women in Kent

Suffragists marching round Hyde Park Corner

Men first!

A cartoon showing a sinking ship with women and children waiting on the sloping deck to be rescued appeared on the front cover of *The Common Cause* late in July. The caption read:

> Mate: What about these women and children?
>
> Captain [bearing a fair resemblance to Lloyd George]: Send off the men first. If there are any boats left, the women can have them.[16]

This caption refers to something Lloyd George had said in the House of Commons a few days before, but in view of what happened on RMS *Titanic* nine months later it has a somewhat prophetic quality.

Dover sea front in about 1913

1911 and 1912
Open-air meetings

In July and August 1911, Miss F Macaulay, late of Somerville College, Oxford, held a number of open-air meetings in Dover to rally support for the Conciliation Bill, which was to extend the parliamentary franchise to women householders who already held the municipal vote.

At a meeting in the Market Square Miss Macaulay "had a considerable amount of interruption from a number of sailors, who were a bit 'lively', and from a number of boys, who were continually shouting insults and, in some cases, obscene remarks to the speaker".[17] At another meeting on the sea-front Miss Hilda Burkett, a visitor from Birmingham, told the audience about her personal experience of prison and force-feeding. Miss Macaulay drew attention to what Mrs Pankhurst described as "cuckoo tactics" – the attempt by some to "wreck the Suffrage Bill by substituting for it one giving votes also to all married women i.e. two votes for every household, which it was certain the House of Commons would never pass".[18]

In July 1911 Mrs Pethick-Lawrence spoke at a WSPU meeting in the Granville Hall in Ramsgate. The other speaker was Mr Hugh Franklin who had recently achieved some notoriety by committing an extraordinary assault on Mr Winston Churchill. Mrs Pethick-Lawrence thanked Ramsgate Council for passing the following resolution: "That this council approves of the Parliamentary Franchise (Women's) Bill for enfranchisement of women householders and urges the government to grant facilities for its passage into law this session," and claimed that women were making sacrifices to obtain the vote "because they were profoundly dissatisfied with the position of women and the position of womanhood in this country".[19] Mrs Pethick-Lawrence also spoke at the Theatre Royal in Margate.

When Emmeline Pethick-Lawrence read about the arrest and imprisonment of Christabel Pankhurst and Annie Kenney in October 1905, she decided to join the WSPU. Not long afterwards Emmeline was arrested and sent to prison for trying to make a speech in the lobby of the House of Commons. In 1907 Emmeline and her husband Frederick started the journal *Votes for Women* and their home in London became the office of the WSPU. In 1912 the WSPU organised a new campaign that involved the large-scale smashing of shop-windows. The moleskin stole and muff shown above would have cost 5 guineas.

Women in Kent

The large muff would have been ideal for hiding a hammer in. Frederick and Emmeline Pethick-Lawrence were arrested, tried and sentenced to nine months' imprisonment. On their release from prison the Pethick-Lawrences were expelled from the WSPU for speaking out openly against the window-smashing campaign.

Emmeline Pethick-Lawrence continued to work for the suffrage cause after 1912, writing for *Votes for Women*. During the First World War she was a prominent member of the Women's International League for Peace and after the passing of the Qualification of Women Act in 1918 she was one of sixteen unsuccessful women candidates that stood in the post-war election.

Summer campaign to increase circulation

In August 1911 A. Maude Royden outlined the campaign for increasing the circulation of *The Common Cause* during the holiday season. She suggests a number of different ways that free copies of the newspaper could be distributed to advertise their cause.

> They might be put in the reading-rooms of hotels, in railway station waiting-rooms and free libraries.
>
> All women's clubs might be approached with a specimen copy and asked to become regular subscribers.
>
> The chief doctors and dentists in each locality might be approached and asked the same, or if not, if they will consent to allow a copy to be sent to them to place on waiting-room tables.
>
> Railway bookstalls might be asked to have them on trial.
>
> Men's clubs might be asked to subscribe, specimen copies being sent at first.

She had asked those societies on the NU list which were situated in holiday resorts whether they would undertake to distribute a certain number of "*Common Causes*" during the six holiday weeks beginning 3rd August, and, if possible, to extend the six weeks to seven, "as the holiday season goes on at least till the middle of September". Readers were reminded that "the papers must be taken (not posted) to the various waiting-rooms, hotels etc., and some member of the Society should make herself personally responsible for seeing that this is done".[20]

Two weeks later *The Common Cause* reported that many dozens of their newspapers had been sold on the beach at Aldeburgh in Suffolk. The reporter then claimed that "If this can be done at Aldeburgh, it could be done at all the seaside places".[21]

An article in the *Dover Times* informed readers of a new sixpenny book published by the Women's Co-operative Guild entitled *Working Women and Divorce*. The book consisted of evidence given on behalf of the Women's Co-operative Guild before the Divorce Commission using the words of the women themselves. They were preparing a report to highlight the inconsistencies of the divorce law as it stood in 1911.[22]

In September 1911 Mrs Elizabeth Knight of Hampstead was charged with defacing the pavement of the Broadway in Broadstairs by chalking "Women's Freedom League – Meeting today at 5.15, just beyond the jetty; Mrs Martyn" on 24th August. "The Cinque Ports Magistrates at Margate imposed a fine of 7

1911 and 1912

shillings. It was the first prosecution of the kind under the new county council bye laws."

On 5th October 1911 Miss Vida Goldstein (*right*), leader of the Women's Movement in Australia, spoke at St George's Hall in Canterbury.[23] Then in December she spoke at the Town Hall in Folkestone. Following her success in obtaining the vote for the women of Victoria in 1909 she had been invited over to England by the WSPU. She had taken part in the Women's Coronation Procession on 17th June and had now formed a committee of ladies from the Colonies to help their sisters in the Mother Country who were still fighting for the right to vote. Miss Clemence Housman, the sister of the writer Laurence Housman, spoke of her imprisonment in Holloway for tax resistance.[24]

The Actresses' Franchise League came to Dover at the end of October to put on an "entertainment" at the Town Hall. The proceedings opened with Miss Victoria Drummond reciting Laurence Housman's 'Prologue'. This was followed by two plays and a string quartet. The first play, *Before the Sunrise*, was set in 1867, where Mr and Mrs Sewell were discussing their daughter's future. Mr Sewell was not happy about the amendment proposed by the newly elected MP John Stuart Mill which was to include women in the franchise. He wanted his daughter to marry her wealthy suitor but she did not love him and wanted to continue her education. The second play, *How the Vote Was Won*, was a farce written by Cicely Hamilton and Mr Christopher St John. This play was set in the future and tells how the suffragettes organise a general strike of women.[25]

On 7th November 1911 Asquith made it quite clear that women's suffrage would not become a government measure while he was Prime Minister, but that the Manhood Suffrage Reform Bill would not affect the chances of the private member's Conciliation Bill. On 24th November, at a Liberal rally in Bath, Lloyd George admitted that "we have torpedoed the Conciliation Bill".

The Common Cause reported that, at a meeting in Ramsgate on 24th November 1911, Chrystal Macmillan had spoken about the Insurance Bill. The secretary reported that there was a majority of suffragists on Ramsgate Town Council!

On 21st November leaders of the woman suffrage movement tried to gain access to the House of Parliament to present a protest against the Government's promised Manhood Suffrage Bill. Denied access, hundreds of women went through the West End smashing windows.

> At Whitehall the police cordon was so strong that all hope of breaking through was impossible. Groups hurled themselves against the police, and in all 223 arrests were made, among the names being Mrs Pethick-Lawrence, Lady Constance Lytton, the Hon Evelyn Haverfield, Mrs Brailsford, and Miss Patricia Woodcock. Two men were also arrested.
>
> Organised damage to public and private property formed part of the tactics pursued by the women. While the attention of the police was occupied in

protecting the House of Commons from members of a deputation which set out from a meeting of Suffragettes in Caxton Hall skirmishing bands of women made sudden window-breaking raids of Government offices and private buildings in different parts of the West-End.

Along Whitehall and Parliament Street stones were hurled through windows of the War Office, Admiralty, Treasury, Home Office, The Local Government Board, The Scottish Office, (Somerset House, the offices of the *Daily Mail*, *Daily News* and Swan & Edgar's department store). The premises of the National Liberal Club, the Liberal Federation, a private bank, and the London and North-Western railway depot suffered in a like manner. Although these raids took the police by surprise, reinforcements were hastily hurried to the various localities, and in most the perpetrators were arrested.[26]

Many suffragists did not agree with the window-smashing campaign and some like Dr Elizabeth Garrett Anderson left the WSPU at this time.

Her sister Mrs Millicent Garrett Fawcett had been granted an interview with the Prime Minister Mr Asquith on 25th November 1911. The NUWSS reported that he had answered in the affirmative to the following questions:

Is it the intention of the Government that the Reform Bill shall go through all its stages in 1912?

Will the Bill be drafted in such a way as to admit of any amendments introducing women on other terms than men?

Will the Government undertake not to oppose such amendments?

Will the Government regard any amendment enfranchising the women which is carried as an integral part of the Bill, and defend it in all its stages?[27]

On 6th December 1911 the Women's Local Government Society was founded in Ramsgate.

1912

The NUWSS abandoned its non-party policy in 1912 and entered into an electoral pact with the Labour Party, which took the form of its Election Fighting Fund. On March 28th the Conciliation Bill was defeated in the House of Commons by only 14 votes. In October the Pethick-Lawrences were asked to leave the WSPU as they could not approve the new militant policy.

In February 1912 a Fabian Society resolution declared that "no measure will be acceptable which does not include both men and women"; and urged government to introduce genuine measure of adult suffrage.[28]

Following Lloyd George's "torpedoing" of the Conciliation Bill in November 1911, Mrs Pankhurst declared in February 1912 that "The argument of the broken pane of glass is the most valuable argument in modern politics".

In February 1912 the Ramsgate branch of the NUWSS passed a resolution deploring the window-smashing activities of WSPU.

Labour Party, ILP and Fabian Society held a demonstration at the Royal Albert Hall in London on 13th February to demand adult suffrage. Speakers included Will Crooks MP. Keir Hardie MP and Philip Snowden MP. The Meeting was chaired by Ramsay Macdonald MP.

Tontine Street in Folkestone in about 1911

On 1st March 1912 suffragettes in the West End drew hammers and stones from their muffs and broke scores of shop and office windows. Over 120 women were arrested. A guerilla campaign ensued, telegraph wires were cut, pillar boxes set on fire, and the homes of government ministers bombed. *Votes for Women* reported that *The Globe* newspaper had coined a new word by describing the suffragettes who were smashing windows in the West End as "Vitrifragists" or glassbreakers. On the following day the *Daily Mail* said: "When the shutters come down this morning in the West End of London they will expose such a sorry show of patched and plastered shop fronts as was never seen since plate glass was invented."[29] On 29th March the Executive Committee of the Fabian Society carried the following resolution: "The Fabian Society protests against the unwise and unnecessary severity of the sentences recently passed on the militant suffragists."

The *Thanet Times* reported that Mr Norman Craig, Thanet's MP, had actually booked a passage on the maiden voyage of RMS *Titanic*, but had changed his mind the day before she sailed and gone golfing instead![30] This poem attributed to Henry Van Dyke appeared later in the year in a programme for a fund-raising concert in New York in aid of a women's memorial to thank the men who drowned. The Guggenheims, who had lost Sir Benjamin in the disaster, were patronesses of the fund.

Heroes of the Titanic
Honour the brave who sleep
Where the lost Titanic lies
The men who knew what a man must do
When he looks death in the eyes

'Women and children first'
Ah! Strong and tender cry!
The sons whom women had borne and nursed
Remembered – and dared to die

The boats crept off in the dark
The great ship groaned: and then
O stars of the night, who saw that sight,
Bear witness, these were men!

Women in Kent

On 24th April 1912 Henrietta Quimby, a 25-year-old journalist from the United States, became the first woman to fly solo across the Channel from Deal to Cap Gris Nez near Calais.

On 25th June 1912 six compartments of a Tunbridge Wells to Victoria train were badly vandalised. This was believed to be the work of suffragettes.[31]

On 12th July 1912, during the debate about the second reading of the Reform Bill, Mr Asquith, the Prime Minister, said: "This Bill does not propose to confer the franchise on women; whatever extensions of the franchise it makes are to male persons only."

On 14th July 1912 George Lansbury MP resigned his parliamentary seat in the East End of London and sought re-election on the single issue of VOTES FOR WOMEN – but he lost his seat!

In August 1912 militant suffragettes tried to find Mr Winston Churchill who was staying at Mr Astor's house in Sandwich. Lady cyclists rode into the road in front of his car, addressed him on the question in which they were interested, and then the car drove away.

A Punch cartoon of 23rd October 1912 shows a young girl sulking and defiant at table. Her mother has just come home and is talking to the nurse.

Mamma: Dear, dear, have I come home to a naughty little girl?

Nurse: Really madam, I don't know what to do with Miss Mabel. She's been very troublesome all the afternoon and now she says if she can't have cake before her bread-and-butter she'll go on hunger strike.

In another cartoon in the same issue, a little boy getting ready for bed is anxious to devise some method of detaining his mother so he says: "Mummy, just stay a little and tell me all about women's suffrage!"

When the Pethick-Lawrences left the WSPU in October 1912, *Votes for Women* became the newspaper of the non-violent suffragists, while Christabel Pankhurst became the editor of the new WSPU newspaper, *The Suffragette*.

In December 1912 several incidences reported in the local newspapers, of tar and other substances being poured into pillar boxes in Thanet, were thought to be the work of militant suffragists.

One of the charming hats recommended for wearing at the Coronation Procession in London advertised by Derry and Toms in June 1911 in the suffragette newspaper Votes for Women.

1911 and 1912

1. VW 20th January 1911
2. KGCP 4th February 1911
3. DTEKG 24th February 1911
4. DTEKG 26th May 1911
5. TGEKA 25th February 1911
6. DTEKG 10th March 1911
7. KGCP 18th March 1911
8. CC 27th April 1911
9. KGCP March 11th 1911
10. DE 3rd March 1911
11. KGCP June 10th 1911
12. TT 16th June 1911
13. CC 15th June 1911
14. KGCP 24th June 1911
15. FH 24th June 1911
16. CC 27th July 1911
17. DE 14th July 1911
18. DE 4th August 1911
19. TT 15th July 1911
20. CC 3rd August 1911
21. CC 17th August 1911
22. DTEKG 18th August 1911
23. KGCP 30th Sept 1911
24. DE 3rd November 1911
25. DE October 27th 1911
26. TGEKA 25th November 1911
27. FH 25th November 1911
28. CC 1st February 1912
29. VW 8th March 1912
30. TT 19th April 1912
31. www.btp.police.uk

Chapter Nine

January–June 1913

> Over one thousand women have gone to prison in the course of this agitation, have suffered their imprisonment, have come out of prison injured in health, weakened in body, but not in spirit. (Emmeline Pankhurst, speech to the Court, 2nd April 1913)

1913 was a very busy year for the suffrage campaign. The withdrawal of suffrage amendments in Parliament in January heralded a new wave of militant protests or "guerrilla warfare" from the suffragettes. The "Cat and Mouse Bill" was introduced in March, and during the summer the non-militant women's pilgrimage toured Kent before taking part in the final event in London.

Evelyn Billing, organizer of the Canterbury WSPU, welcomed the Archbishop's reference to the Woman Suffrage Movement in his sermon on 29th December but added that

> I wish that the Archbishop had not fallen into the common error of speaking of militancy as "precipitancy". Women and their men champions have been working for the vote ever since the middle of the last century; surely we are not precipitate. The fact is that the general public has got into the habit of thinking that the agitation only began with the initiation of "militant" methods in 1905.[1]

Hilda Stainer, Folkestone's Honorary Press Secretary for the NUWSS, wrote to the editor to inform readers of the important amendment to the Reform Bill, proposed by Sir Edward Grey, which would remove the word "male", due to come before Parliament on the evening of Monday 27th January.

> The other important amendments in favour of woman suffrage are tabled for divisions as follows:-
>
> On Monday at 10.30pm – the adult suffrage amendment
>
> On Tuesday January 28th at 7.30pm the Dickinson amendment, which aims at the enfranchisement of women householders and the wives of men occupiers
>
> On Tuesday 28th January at 10.30pm, the "Conciliation" amendment, which would enfranchise women householders.
>
> There is good ground for hoping that Sir E Grey's amendment will obtain a majority, and it will then be left to the House of Commons to vote upon the other amendments without pressure from the Party Whips.
>
> Local suffragists are glad to remember that Sir Philip Sassoon gave a signed pledge to support woman suffrage in the House of Commons upon his election for the borough of Hythe last year. A resolution in favour of women suffrage has also been passed by the Folkestone Town Council.

A *Punch* cartoon of 15th January 1913 shows a man sitting in underground train. A lady is standing up next to him. He tells her she is standing on his feet. The lady replies: "If you were anything of a man you'd be standing on them yourself!"

Women in Kent

All supporters of the enfranchisement of women – without regard to party politics, are invited to assist the cause during the next few days, by using their personal influence with members, or by sending letters and telegrams to members at the House of Commons in support of the various amendments.[2]

Lloyd George was also in favour of this amendment. On 27th January, however, the Speaker of the House of Commons ruled that the women's suffrage amendments would necessitate a whole new Bill being drawn up and the Bill was withdrawn. That same evening Mrs Charlotte Despard was arrested for holding a protest meeting in Trafalgar Square. Mrs Pankhurst declared guerilla warfare and a new period of militant protests began.

Mrs Pankhurst said that the women leaders had shown as much heroism, resource, and ingenuity as any of the great men who had waged guerrilla warfare in the past. "It was guerilla warfare that they declared that afternoon. (Loud cheers)" She declared that "as soon as they knew exactly what had happened in the House of Commons that afternoon they would hold a Council of War, and decide when to begin proceedings". She hoped that Cabinet members who supported women suffrage would do their duty and resign.[3]

Charlotte Despard was arrested and imprisoned for her WSPU activities, but in 1907 she helped to form the Women's Freedom League, which still took a militant approach but only used non-violent illegal methods to promote women's suffrage. She was a pacifist so in 1914 refused to become involved in the army's recruitment campaign, despite the fact that her brother was Sir John French, Chief of Staff of the British Army.

Beatrice Oetzmann, who was descended from a German family, married Harry Chapman when she was 32 years old in 1895. Harry was manager of a watermill in Hertfordshire but Beatrice felt that the damp river valley was an unhealthy place to bring up her two daughters so for quite long periods she would bring the girls to live by the sea in Margate. She was a strong character and rather eccentric, who was fiercely argumentative about the "superiority of women". While in Margate she threw herself wholeheartedly into the work of the local suffrage society. Her grand-daughter was put in touch with me through staff at Margate Library while I was writing this book and kindly supplied biographical details and several photographs of her grandmother.

A *Punch* cartoon of 29th January 1913 entitled, "Another injustice to women", featured ladies queuing to go in to the House of Commons. They see a new notice which says "LADIES' GALLERY – SILENCE!" An indignant female chorus replies that they will soon alter that!

Throughout 1913, and up until the outbreak of war in 1914, Beatrice Chapman, in her capacity as Honorary Secretary of the Margate branch of the NUWSS, wrote almost weekly to the local papers on matters concerning women's issues and their suffrage campaign.

January–June 1913

*Beatrice and Harry Chapman and their daughter Muriel in about 1897
(by kind permission of Diana Spence)*

At the AGM of the Women's Liberal Association in Ramsgate the secretary's report stated that the Association had contributed £22 to the men's fund, and that made them wonder whether they were always going to be "hewers of wood and drawers of water to the men's association, always providing funds but receiving nothing in return. They thought it was high time the Liberal Party made the cause of women's suffrage one of the foremost planks of their programme."[4]

Six windows at Lambeth were smashed by "a lady Suffragette", Miss Henrietta Hunt of Itchen near Southampton. She spent fourteen days in Holloway prison because she refused to be bound over.[5] In February, railwaymen from East Kent participated in an imaginary suffragette riot during their annual competitions. Deal came first, Faversham second, and Ramsgate third!

The *Folkestone Baptist* magazine for February contained the following paragraph:

> We regret that the action of the ladies leading the campaign on behalf of the enfranchisement of women makes it necessary for many who support the movement to stand in opposition because of the methods pursued. We hear that Folkestone is to have its "outrage". We do not know whether it is to be letter burning, window smashing or breaking up public meetings, but either will only cause damage to the cause and provide another reason for keeping women out of politics.

Miss Hilda Stainer of the Folkestone NUWSS was keen to point out that the militant suffragists were "a small, though zealous and noisy section" and that the "thousands of law-abiding men and women who comprise the other Suffrage Societies" made up the majority of the campaigners. She had not personally heard of any planned "outrages" but the NUWSS did not agree with violence.[6]

Women in Kent

Women in a church parade in Burgate in Canterbury in about 1911

A front page cartoon in *Votes for Women* at the end of February suggested that the government dealt with militancy by mistaking the symptom for the disease. A Dr "Asquith" says to Britannia, who is suffering from internal disorder, that he does not like the look of her tongue and proposes to cut it out.[7]

In the same issue was the following article claiming that the suffragettes' militant campaign had cost the nation £500,000 in the last seven years:

> The losses are roughly set under three heads:-
>> Actual damage caused by wanton outrage
>>
>> Heavy expense of preventing and detecting outrage, a sum larger than most people suspect
>>
>> The withdrawal of funds from charitable and other public purposes by women who are supporting the movement
>
> The following are some of the more recent items:-
>> Bomb explosion at Chancellors' house – cost £500 to £600
>>
>> Richmond Park pavilion burnt out – £700
>>
>> Kew pavilion burned down £1,000 (or more)
>>
>> Golf greens damaged – over £100
>>
>> Letters damaged and telegraph wires cut, costs not yet ascertained
>
> This excludes the cost of surveillance.[8]

Votes for Women describes some of the reported attacks on pillar boxes and telegraph wires.

> A number of pillar boxes have been attacked in various parts of the country. For instance, considerable damage was caused at Bradford last Thursday,

January-June 1913

where black fluid was poured into the main letter box. On Friday, again, upwards of a hundred letters were damaged at Oxford by an inky substance, and green paint in a tube was also put into the letter box at Charing Cross Post Office. On the same day it is alleged that an unknown Suffragist dropped an explosive phial into the Inland Revenue Department's letter box at Birmingham, which at the time contained paper money to the value of £5,000. When the phial exploded, however, the post office officials claim that they managed to save the contents of the box.

Telegraph wires to the north of Kenton, Newcastle, were found on Friday afternoon to have been cut. The damage was attributed to Suffragists, as on a label attached to a telegraph pole was found the strange device "Votes for Women".[9]

A former Margate suffragist, Mrs Lewis, had moved to Calgary in Canada where she had just set up a Women's Suffrage Society. A former member of the WSPU, Mrs Lewis was asked about the militants. She replied:

> Yes, I am a militant suffragette. For years I belonged to the other faction of suffragettes, but I got so disheartened and discouraged with the little accomplished, that I joined the militants. They are the ones in England who have done the real work. There is a great deal of work to be done in Alberta but I think Canadian women will obtain the franchise much easier than English women, for undoubtedly Canadian men do treat women more as equals.[10]

On 10th March 1913 five suffragettes tried to petition King at the opening of Parliament but did not get near his coach.

At the AGM of NUWSS in Ramsgate, Miss Griffith-Jones, who was working as organizer for the Kent Federation, spoke of the increased prosperity of the women's suffrage movement in Kent, and of the formation of new societies in Rochester, Canterbury and Margate, the last being an offshoot of the Ramsgate Society. It should be noted in the society's report that the "Friends of Woman Suffrage" scheme had also been set up in Ramsgate for the enrolment of sympathisers, who do not wish to become members of the society.[11]

> A *Punch* cartoon with the caption "The Suspected Sex" was reproduced in Canterbury's local paper in March 1913. The stationmaster-cum-porter of a wayside "Halt" is calling up to his mate Bill in the signalbox. A little old lady can be seen in the distance sitting on a bench waiting for a train.
> Stationmaster: *"Ere Bill, just keep an eye on the old gal on the platform whilst I gets my dinner."*
> Bill: *"Whoffor? She can't come to no harm."*
> Stationmaster: *"I'm not thinkin' of 'er 'ealth. I'm thinkin' about my station. She might want to burn it down."*[1]

In March the "Cat and Mouse Bill" was introduced or, to give it its correct title, the Prisoners' Temporary Discharge for Ill-Health Act (3 Geo V c.4). Reginald McKenna, who was Home Secretary, argued that the suffragettes had 'declared war on society' and that this measure would reduce the disgusting practice of forcible feeding. Keir Hardie opposed the Bill as futile and unfair. Lord Robert Cecil suggested deportation instead. Mrs Pankhurst was arrested twelve times under the Cat and Mouse Act.

Ramsgate beach with the new Royal Victoria Pavilion and a number of bathing machines in about 1909. The woman wearing an apron might be one of the dippers who used to help bathers get into the sea.

A few weeks later in a single day, the Bill was rushed through its second and third readings in the House of Lords. Although the Lord Chancellor regretted that the Bill should be necessary, he claimed that: "it was notoriously directed against a certain class of prisoners – women who had committed acts of violence and had been properly sentenced," although he conceded that "they were actuated by no sordid or personal motive, but believed they were fighting for their liberties." Lord Salisbury said that the Opposition reluctantly agreed to the Bill but did not feel it was "the proper way of passing legislation affecting the liberties of the subject".[12]

It was not always women who were force-fed, however. In the same edition of *The Suffragette* is a letter from Hugh Franklin, who had been force-fed 114 times in Wormwood Scrubs prison. His letter describing his experiences in "the Cat-and-Mouse-trap" had been read out at a meeting on 29th April where Mrs Pethick-Lawrence and Mr Israel Zangwil spoke against force-feeding, and Mr Scurr from the Dockers' Union made "a passionate appeal" for free speech. Mr Zangwil had also spoken at a meeting of the Tax Resistance League. He claimed that "The question before them" (i.e. the Government attitude on taxation and representation) sounded like "Alice in Wonderland, but it was really **Asquith in Blunderland**".[13]

Militancy and otherwise

Sarah Kingsley, the Honorary Secretary of the Hythe NUWSS reported that the NUWSS had gained 12,000 new members in the last year, bringing the total membership up to 43,000.

January-June 1913

Besides the NUWSS there are the New Constitutional Society and about thirty other non-militant societies, possibly more. It is well for this to be clearly understood, for in various directions, either from ignorance or malice, it is being industriously circulated that all suffragists are militants, of course, quite inaccurately.[14]

In the same paper a male correspondent asked whether "men can afford to throw stones at the militant women" considering that in the past British politicians have "constantly refused to listen to any cry that was not accompanied by disorder, riot, and violence". He then quotes six examples including the Second Reform Bill "which was not passed until the railings in Hyde Park were pulled down by the mob".[15] He suggested that it was hardly surprising that suffragettes have used the same tactics since they seemed to work for men in the past.

Miss Lynette Griffiths-Jones (Organizing Secretary of Kentish Federation of NUWSS) wrote to the *Thanet Times* on 4th April 1913 about Mrs Despard's recent lecture on the "White Slave Traffic and Sweated Industries", at the Foresters' Hall in Margate, in which she urged the audience to join one of the suffrage societies working to obtain political freedom for women and to put a stop to these practices.

She also urged readers to join the newly formed Margate branch of the NUWSS, of which Mrs Henry Fawcett (widow of the late blind Postmaster-General) was President.

The Canterbury newspaper reported that "a Reuter telegram from Boston (USA) states that Miss Florence Ward, a Birmingham suffragist, was debarred from landing on the ground that she was sentenced in London to four months' imprisonment for taking part in the window-breaking movement". She was expected to appeal against this decision![16]

A sweated industries and women's suffrage exhibition was held at the Town Hall in Folkestone in April 1913. Mrs Flora Annie Steel who presided at the opening ceremony claimed that they had to look at the future of women and of women's interests "which was a far more serious question than all the votes in the world". She said she wore the badge of the "spiritual militant" who carried no stone in her hands or matches in her pocket but had sworn she would not sit still and see women starving.[17]

Another new word

Yet again the national press came up with another new word to describe the militant tactics of the suffragettes.

> A new kind of woman has been created by the present Government, and the sooner she disappears the better for law and order and national dignity. This new woman is the Outragette. She began simply as one asking that women should have votes. Later she became a Suffragette and then a Militant, and finally, exasperated by the pettifogging evasions which are possible under our so-called system of representative government, she became an Outragette, a window-smasher, a rioter, wrecker, and incendiary.[18]

Women in Kent
Mrs Rackham visits East Kent

The first public meeting of the newly formed Margate branch of NUWSS was held at Forrester's Hall on 14th April when Mrs Rackham, a Poor Law Guardian in Cambridge, and a member of the National Executive of the Women's Suffrage Societies, gave a lecture on "Why Women need the Vote".

A male reporter for the *Thanet Times* referred to his description of the meeting as "the impressions of a mere man".

> It was comparatively tame. The one policeman at the door was quite apologetic when he desired me to produce for inspection the contents of a bulging overcoat pocket. It was found to consist of a well-filled tobacco pouch and a note book. The custodian of the law even refrained from annexing the former, and he looked disdainfully at the latter.

He thought it was "a rather dull evening" but added that

> ... those of us who were too abashed to look this unrelenting clever woman orator in the face, and stand up and give her a Roland for an Oliver, buried our blushing, shamed countenances in some of the literature which was plentifully scattered around. We read fourteen of the many thousands of reasons why women think that some of them should enjoy that priceless privilege of the vote.[19]

'A Roland for an Oliver' meant having an answer for everything, or blow-by-blow retaliation. In this context it could also mean heckling the speaker.

Mrs Rackham said there were four reasons why the women's demand for the vote was opposed.

> It was thought (1) that they wanted government by women: whereas what they really wanted was co-operation between men and women. (2) That women would be out of place as voters: but the women were starting to feel that while they were preparing the children for the world they needed to take their full share in preparing the world for the children – a task which men could not accomplish satisfactorily alone. (3) That the demand was inseparably connected with violence: but the oldest and largest Women's Suffrage Society was absolutely constitutional in its methods, as were nearly all the other thirty Societies. (4) That it was a new demand: but many of the spheres and occupations now accepted as suitable for women had been opposed on the same ground.

Mrs Rackham also spoke at St George's Hall in Canterbury on 15th April and at a meeting of the Ramsgate branch of the NUWSS at Cave's Café in Broadstairs. She claimed,

> ... that the granting of the vote to women would be good for the country, for the good of men and for the good of women as well. It would give an all-round benefit. Personally she had nothing to say against the militant section of the suffragettes, but her own belief was in the adoption of constitutional methods. In countries where women had been given the vote they had received that privilege by means of constitutional agitation and not by the adoption of militant methods.[20]

January–June 1913

Miss Macaulay arrested

Miss F Macaulay, area organizer for the South Kent WSPU was arrested for obstructing the police. She had been acting a "patrol" outside Holloway prison. When the police asked her to go away she refused so she was arrested. She was found guilty and fined £5. She chose to go to prison rather than pay the fine, but within an hour an anonymous friend had paid the fine and Miss Macaulay was released.[21]

"Within the last few weeks the Suffragette outrages have increased in number and daring and no class of property has been immune from attack." The previous Friday the pavilion on the Nevill Cricket Ground in Tunbridge Wells was burnt down. The building was insured but the greater loss was the valuable collection of sporting trophies including a fine print of the first cricket week at Canterbury.[22]

Why working women should be enfranchised

In April 1913 organizations such as the Women's Co-operative Guild, the Fabian Women's Group and the Women's Labour League joined forces to present another petition to Parliament on behalf of the 35,000 working women who were still excluded from the rights of citizenship.

The text of the resolution gave five reasons why working women should be enfranchised:

> Because women as wage earners occupy a weaker position in the industrial world than men and therefore especially require the protection of the vote in dealing with industrial legislation affecting women workers.
>
> Because the majority of married working women who are not wage earners are deeply concerned as wage spenders in all industrial legislation and in such social questions as taxation, education, housing and land reform.
>
> Because the lives of women are greatly affected by questions of national service, and foreign policy, and they should therefore have a voice therein as citizens.
>
> Because so long as women are excluded from the counsels of the nation their capacity for public service is lost to the State.
>
> Because justice demands political freedom for men and women alike, and the refusal of it to working women hinders them in the struggle they are daily waging to raise the burdens of poverty from their homes and gain a happier future for their children.[23]

Even though the Government had banned the suffragettes from holding outdoor meetings in 1913, many attempts were made to flout the ban. A report in *The Suffragette* describes one such occasion where: "In spite of dismal skies and threatening clouds thousands of people assembled in Hyde Park on Sunday afternoon" to see if the militant women would appear. Eventually the patience of the crowd was awarded as WSPU banner was suddenly unfurled in a wide green space near the entrance gate. The crowd stampeded in that direction and a woman addressed the crowd, cheered on by shouts of "Free speech!" from her audience. The police started to rush the crowd "with an utter disregard of any injury they might inflict upon individuals in the process" or any attempt to protect the women from the rough hooligan element in the crowd. "In several instances it was solely due to the intervention of decent-minded men that women who were taking no part in the struggle escaped severe hustling at the hands of the roughs."[24]

In the same paper was an article reporting that many of the trades unions had passed resolutions condemning Home Secretary Reginald McKenna's attempt to prevent free speech in the parks.

In April and May incidents were reported in the local press of hoax bombs placed by local youths in Minster and Margate Stations, one inside a copy of *The Suffragette* so that militant suffragists would get the blame. Suffragettes trying to sell their newspapers along the seafront at Cliftonville on Whit Monday were hooted at by visitors. This sort of behaviour led Broadstairs Council to decline an application for a suffrage meeting at the Bandstand in June.

This intriguing article appeared in the *Folkestone Herald* in May 1913:

Was she a suffragette?

One evening recently a woman was seen loitering about in the vicinity of the grounds of Cheriton Council, which are situated near the outskirts of the populated part of the district. She was wearing a purple hat, green veil and a cream coat, the colours of the suffragettes. The stranger asked if the building was the labour Exchange Bureau, and as she did not quit the vicinity she was asked to leave.[25]

A letter to editor of the *Thanet Times* from "A Member of the NUWSS" was headed "Why Women want the Vote".

Having read with interest the Anti-Suffrage leaflet "Who are the Suffragists" under your heading "Opinions from various standpoints on questions of the moment", perhaps you will kindly give publicity to the opinions of the Suffragists themselves on the question of "Who are the Suffragists".

They are women who think that as they are human beings and also citizens they should, by every principle of justice, have the same political rights and protection as men.

They are women too who see that it is absolutely necessary for the well-being of the State, that the women's point of view should be considered in the laws which touch her at every point in her life, as women's well-being is so intimately mixed up with men's, that which injures the one, must of necessity affect the other injuriously in the long run.[26]

In May the second reading of Mr Dickinson's Representation of the People (Women) Bill, which asked for the enfranchisement of women householders and the wives of householders, was rejected by the House of Commons. The Canterbury MP supported the amendment.[27]

Prohibition of indoor meetings

Encouraged by the prohibition of open-air meetings, the owners of halls in London began to ban militant suffragists from holding indoor meetings too. The Essex Hall was forbidden to the WSPU, and even to the Clerks' WSPU, an association of women clerks, mostly employed in the City, who tried to hire the hall for a meeting there on 19th May. Similar difficulties were experienced in suburban halls and the WFL were refused permission to use Caxton Hall on the grounds that "violent militant speeches" were made there at a recent meeting held by the League: "This statement, on inquiry, appeared to have been made on the authority of a newspaper account, which was said to have alleged that subscriptions were asked for at the meeting for the placing of bombs in houses and churches. The WFL, who have never advocated the destruction of property in any form, are demanding the production of the newspaper report in question."[28]

This anonymous "snippet" appeared in the *Thanet Times* in May:

> Basking in the sun hundreds of people made al fresco meals on the seashore. The luncheon basket was as much in evidence as ever. Scores of happy children paddled and built wonderful sand castles while their parents nodded under the chalk cliffs and read of the latest outrages by the militant suffragettes.[29]

A house in West Folkestone called Highlands was partially destroyed by fire and the work was attributed to the suffragettes as postcards relating to women's suffrage were found in the vicinity. Luckily the house was uninhabited at the time of the fire but the main staircase was completely destroyed and £1,000 worth of damage was caused.[30] A plain postcard addressed to the "Right Dishonourable Prime Minister" was found with a number of quotations apparently pasted on the back, including one by Charlotte Bronte: "People hate to be reminded of ills they are unable or unwilling to remedy: such reminder troubles their ease and shakes their self-complacency." Two photos of the damage caused appeared in the paper under the heading "Wild Women's Work" but the quality was too poor for them to be reproduced here.[31]

Another letter to the editor from Beatrice Chapman (Hon Sec NUWSS Margate branch) to inform readers that:

> Among the 100 odd Bills which have been, or still are, before the House of Commons this session there are many besides the various Franchise Bills which concern women so intimately that it is inconceivable that they can be properly considered in all their bearings by an assembly composed entirely of men. There is the Cottage Homes for Aged Persons Bill, a Divorce Bill, two Government Bills dealing with the elementary education of defective and epileptic children and the employment of children, two Bills for the housing of working classes, Mr King's Illegitimacy and Maternity Bill, a Bill for the admission of women to the legal profession, a Mental Deficiency Bill, a Nurses' Registration Bill, and a Bill for the repeal of the Vaccination Acts. In questions of housing, education of defective children, employment of children, illegitimacy and maternity and the registration of nurses, surely women are greater experts than men: and in a matter like divorce, which concerns them vitally, surely they are entitled to a hearing![32]

At a meeting at the Liberal Club in Canterbury in May, Miss Griffith Jones told the audience she was well aware that some people had been turned away from supporting the cause by the militants, but she said this was not fair.

> There were over 70,000 constitutional suffragettes, and something like 1,000 militants. The Press had given great publicity to the doings of the militants, but had suppressed the meetings of the constitutionals. They had held over

Women in Kent

20,000 meetings in one year, but little was heard about it. When, however, a few militants broke windows in Oxford Street, within half an hour the whole country knew of it.[33]

> A *Punch* cartoon of 4th June 1913 pictures a rather harassed lady of little means on her knees in front of fireplace. After long and futile efforts to light a fire for her tea-kettle, the militant suffragist says to herself "And to think that only yesterday I burnt two

A letter to the editor from Beatrice Chapman making readers aware that the Scotch Home Rule Bill passed its second reading on the previous Friday, by a small majority of 45, but no provision had been made for the representation of women, despite the fact that all the matters dealt with such as public health and education especially concern women. She added: "And even Anti-Suffragists themselves advocate the extension of women's work in local government".[34]

The following week Beatrice Chapman wrote concerning the report about the Census of 1911 which, she says, "must surely prove to all open-minded persons that there is something radically wrong with our present man-made organization, and it is high time that women were allowed to help where men acting alone have failed to obtain the best results". She then went on to talk about the high infant mortality rates.[35]

On 14th June 1913 Emily Wilding Davison died during the Derby race at Epsom after running out onto the course and attempting to grab the bridle of Anmer, a horse owned by King George V. The horse collided with her and her skull was fractured. She never regained consciousness. Although she did achieve her objective by gaining a lot of publicity for the WSPU, the general public thought she was mentally ill. A splendid funeral procession was organized for Emily by the militant suffragettes. Fragments of film of the incident and the funeral survive.

> A *Punch* cartoon of 25th June 1913 depicts a lady searching in her handbag. An over-zealous policeman suspecting her of concealing a hammer asks her to stop what she is doing and move on. The perfectly innocent young lady replies: "Then perhaps you will kindly blow my nose for me."

The non-militant pilgrimage

A letter from the local officers of the Margate branch of the NUWSS invited "all men and women who are in sympathy with the women's just demands" to attend and help at the local Pilgrimage meetings which would be held at Broadstairs, Ramsgate, Minster and Monkton, Sarre and St Nicholas, Birchington, Herne Bay, Whitstable and Canterbury, where the "Pilgrims" would attend a service at the cathedral at 3pm. They reinforced the message that "the NUWSS does not use violence: its appeal is to reason and the sense of justice".[36]

This description of a suffragette meeting in Broadstairs is almost Dickensian in its turn of phrase :

January-June 1913

> **National Union of Women's Suffrage Societies.**
> **Non-Militant Pilgrimage.**
> OPEN-AIR MEETINGS
> MONDAY, JUNE 30th, 7.30 p.m.,
> THE SQUARE, GARLINGE.
> TUESDAY, JULY 1st,
> **MISS MURIEL MATTERS**
> At CECIL SQUARE, 3.30 and 8 p.m.
> (If wet, at FORESTERS' HALL).
> Pilgrimage starts WEDNESDAY, JULY 2nd,
> CECIL SQUARE, 3.30 p.m.
> For further details apply 2, Lyndhurst Avenue.

Advertisement from the Thanet Times

There is a goodly crowd gathered in the centre of the Broadway. Perched on an insecure-looking stepladder of a platform is a slight girlish figure, while still higher, above her head, the purple, white and green banner floats proudly. The speaker is fair and youthful, which counts for something, but it is the eloquence of her pleading which holds her audience (says a sympathetic writer in the *Daily Citizen*). At first she is subject to many interruptions. Gradually her passionate enthusiasm and her manifest earnestness wear these down.

There is no place for cold, remorseless logic in her presentation of the case. Her periods flow down in a torrent of burning protests and against the injustices which women suffer and in scathing denunciations of the Government and its anti-suffrage members. Her whole being is instinct with zeal, and even the callow, well-dressed youths who have come to scoff forbear for a while their asinine remarks and ribald jests. Overdressed girls, who hitherto have had few thoughts about anything save dress and flirtations, become conscious of disquieting sensations beneath their broad-brimmed hats and low-cut bodices.

Question-time comes. The speaker deals sympathetically with earnest inquiries, and sharply, but lightly, with those of the impertinent order. Then, on her left, a male individual in a cruched felt and skyscraper collar puts what is meant to be a killing question. "How would the speaker like to be a man?" As if stung by an electric needle the speaker faces round to the questioner. A steely glitter lights her eyes, the muscles of the erst-while glowing face grow taut as a bent rapier. For a full half-minute she stays her reply, her eyes meanwhile striving to pierce through the outer wrappings of the masculine person.

Then, in low, but clear, staccato tones, that ring like pistol shots across the silence, comes the retort: "How would you?"[37]

What women think

The hiding of her feelings constitutes half the wisdom of a woman. (Mrs W K Clifford)

A woman has a mind with all sorts of odd corners. She loves details and snippets of things, but give her one big thing to tackle and she's beaten. (Mrs Stanley Wrench)[38]

This charming gown was for sale at Lewis, Hyland and Linom in Ramsgate in May 1913[39]

---

[1] KGCP 11th January 1913
[2] FH 25th January 1913
[3] *Morning Post* 28th January 1913
[4] KGCP 24th January 1913
[5] KGCP 1st February 1913
[6] FH 8th February 1913
[7] VW 28th February 1913
[8] VW 28th February 1913
[9] VW 21st February 1913
[10] TT 7th March 1913
[11] IOTG 13th March 1913
[12] *The Suffragette* 2nd May 1913
[13] Ibid.
[14] FH 29th March 1913
[15] Ibid
[16] KGCP 5th April 1913
[17] FH 5th April 1913
[18] Weekly Dispatch 13th April 1913
[19] TT 18th April 1913
[20] IOTG 19th April 1913
[21] KGCP 19th April 1913
[22] KGCP 19th April 1913
[23] *The Suffragette* 2nd May 1913
[24] Ibid.
[25] FH 3rd May 1913
[26] TT 9th May 1913
[27] KGCP 10th May 1913
[28] VW 16th May 1913

[29] TT 16th May 1913
[30] KGCP 17th May 1913
[31] FH 17th May 1913
[32] IOTG 24th May 1913
[33] KGCP 24th May 1913
[34] IOTG 7th June 1913
[35] IOTG 14th June 1913
[36] IOTG 23rd June 1913
[37] TT 27th June 1913
[38] TT 30th June 1913
[39] TT 9th May 1913

Chapter Ten

July–December 1913

A little old lady is walking past a large house and is delving into her capacious handbag. She says: "Now isn't that provoking? Here's a lovely big house to let and I've forgotten my matches!" (*Punch* cartoon, 2nd July 1913)

Non-militant suffrage pilgrimage

Throughout July there were numerous references to the planned suffrage demonstration which would end in London's Hyde Park on 26th July. This reporter was clearly not very impressed by the organizational skills of the suffragists.

> This plan briefly is that each Federation, comprising in all 400 societies, shall organise a pilgrimage, and march from north, south, east and west to London, joining each other on the way, and also holding meetings, distributing literature, and selling the non-militant newspaper, *Common Cause*. The various Federations will converge, and enter London on Saturday July 26th: they will then proceed to Hyde Park where speakers from at least 20 platforms will address the public.
>
> The Kentish pilgrims started their operations on Monday with a well attended and successful meeting in the Square at Garlinge: and on Tuesday some of them drove through Margate and Westgate in a waggonette, decorated with the National Union's colours to advertise the two open-air meetings in Cecil Square. The first of these meetings took place at 3.30 when Miss Muriel Matters, a young and highly-gifted speaker, held the interest of a more or less sympathetic audience for an hour.
>
> There was another meeting in the square that evening followed by a meeting on Wednesday near the Queen's Bandstand. "The "Pilgrims" proceeded during the afternoon to Broadstairs and Ramsgate, where other meetings were held, and so the pilgrims will make their sad journey till London is reached on July 26th. As far as the Margate and district meetings are concerned, the truthful chronicler is compelled to describe them as unsuccessful verging on a fiasco. But of course, that is the fault of those dreadful suffragettes.1

Muriel Matters was an Australian who came to England in 1905 and joined the Women's Freedom League in 1907. In 1908 she took the first "Votes for Women" horse-drawn caravan on a tour of southern England, and in 1909 scattered leaflets from an airship on the day of the opening of Parliament. In October 1908 Muriel chained herself to a grille in the ladies' gallery of the House of Commons. In 1913 she toured the whole of Kent as a speaker for the NUWSS.

Women in Kent
A Militant

This poem was written by Maude Sansom Carter as a tribute to
Emily Davison, published in *Votes for Women* in July 1913.

Calm days and gentle ease
Her spirit sought for
She, who preferred to these
The cause she fought for

Fragile the strife among
Nothing could bend her
In the foe's face she flung
Her "No Surrender"

Stiff armour of the strife
Still buckled on her
She gave her fighting life
Her Cause to honour.

Woman's station in life

This article reprinted from the *Daily Telegraph* suggesta that a woman's status was seen differently in America.

> We are generally agreed that if a woman is used to purple and fine linen it is a hardship for her to come down to sackcloth. Most of us would allow that a wife may reasonably require her husband to provide her with comfort and luxury according to his income.
>
> Most of us would insist that if, through his fault, she is compelled to leave him, she has a moral claim to maintenance on the standard which obtained while they lived together. All this seems in the nature of platitude to us. But there are different opinions in America. "Her station in life! That sounds very well in novels, but many a woman has to marry a rich man before she has a station in life at all."
>
> This curious utterance comes from Mr Justice Aspinall, of the Supreme Court of Brooklyn, USA. It sounds rather like Sir Peter Teazle in a passion than the measured language of the Bench. "Taste?" quoth Sir Peter, "Zounds! Madam, you had no taste when you married me." "Station in life?" cries the American Bench. "The wife has no station in life except what her husband deigns to give her." Something seems to have happened to the judicial impartiality.[2]

In the same paper was the text of a letter Beatrice Chapman had received from Norman Craig, MP for Thanet, who claimed that he was "in favour of the extension of the franchise to women who are possessed of qualifying property and who are at present without representation direct or indirect" (i.e. through husbands or parents). He was not in favour of full adult suffrage for men or women, and felt that "untold injury has been done to the cause of Women's Suffrage by the wanton crimes of the militant extremists".

Beatrice Chapman also disagreed with the reporter's account of the recent meetings in Cecil Square. She claimed that 159 people had purchased the Society's newspaper *The Common Cause*, 89 people had signed "Friend's cards", and the collection totalled £2/14/6. She also contradicted the assertion that the promoters of the meeting were escorted by the police from the square.

July–December 1913

On Saturday evening a card – to which was attached a heavy weight in the shape of a very large bullet – was found on the handle of the entrance door of the Canterbury Cricket Club. The card bore the words "Votes for Women" and underneath "Canterbury Cricket House". The matter is regarded as a joke on the part of someone, probably a member of the Club, but in view of the outrages which have taken place in the County of late, the local police are keeping a sharp "look out" on all premises.[3]

The South-Kent Pilgrimage

On 11th July 1913 Canterbury was visited by a band of non-militant suffragettes calling themselves the Kentish Pilgrims. There were two routes mapped out in Kent. The northern route began in Margate on 30th June and included Broadstairs, Ramsgate, Minster and Monkton, Sarre and St Nicholas, Birchington and Herne Bay and Whitstable. After Canterbury the Pilgrims would visit Boughton and Faversham, Sittingbourne, Rainham, Newington, Gillingham, Chatham and Rochester before meeting up with the other group at Tonbridge on 21st July. Meetings were held at the Westgate where Miss Muriel Matters addressed a large crowd despite the rain.[4]

The South-Kent Pilgrimage was organized by Miss Ward, assisted by Mrs Abbott (a speaker from NUWSS headquarters) and Mrs Cooke. Hilda Stainer was responsible for organizing the local meetings.

> The pilgrims came to Folkestone from Dover. They have made what they consider a very successful tour of towns in the south-east of the county, and profited greatly by the kindness of Lady Brassey (wife of the Lord Warden of the Cinque Ports) who placed her motor car at their disposal.

The opening gathering at "The Fountain", in Harbour Street in Folkestone, was postponed due to rain.

> There were one or two interruptions. One man mounted the wagon from which the ladies addressed the meeting. He arrogated to himself the position of Chairman, but, as the meeting progressed became so loquacious in the performance of his duties that he was ultimately forcibly removed by the police.[5]

The suffragists also held a meeting in the Market Square in Hythe on 18th July 1913 where a large but orderly and generally sympathetic crowd was addressed by Mrs Henry Kingsley and Mrs Cooke.[6]

Beatrice Chapman wrote to the *Thanet Times* about the coming demonstration in Hyde Park "when our colours of scarlet, white and green will be much in evidence, and thousands of banners will be carried with such words as 'Law-abiding Suffragists', as we now, as always, protest against violence, our motto being 'By Faith, and not by Force'."[7]

On 26th July 1913 200 women from Kent joined the massive "Pilgrimage" organised by the NUWSS in Hyde Park designed to show the Liberal Government how strongly women felt they should have the vote.

A number of anti-suffrage meetings were held during the same week in Cecil Square in Margate. On Tuesday evening a resolution against votes for women was passed by 150 to 8!

Women in Kent

Hilda Stainer of Folkestone NUWSS thanked everyone who had helped with the suffrage pilgrimage.

> Our speakers were given a fair hearing, our paper *The Common Cause* was largely bought, and the crowds appeared to be convinced that the vast majority of women suffragists are entirely innocent of unconstitutional and outrageous methods of promoting their cause.
>
> On behalf of the local branch of the Union, I offer our gratitude to the Press for their valuable assistance in advertising and reporting our meetings, to the Superintendent pf Police and the constables for their kind and courteous supervision, and to the members of the general public who gave us their support at meetings.[8]

In the same paper was this letter concerning women's suffrage.

> Sir – The ladies belonging to the non-militant society who are now promenading the country show clearly by this very action what they owe to the militants, whom, at the same time, they are abusing, for they would never have undertaken even this mild form of advertisement if the militants, by numerous processions and outdoor meetings, had not shown them the way. The defence of all militancy is contained in the undisputed fact that it has familiarised the who population of this country with the claim of "Votes for Women." In the space of a few years, whilst the tactics of the National Union, who had the whole suffrage campaign in their own hands for over forty years, had for its result the fact that the great mass of the people never knew that such a claim was made or that any suffrage society existed.
>
> One of the militant speakers said the other day that she was addressing an outdoor meeting and happened to mention that she had belonged to a suffrage society for forty years, when a voice from the audience shouted out "That's all a lie; They only started six years ago." The militants are quite content to bear all the misunderstanding and abuse of such ignorant persons, as that interruptor; but it does seem rather unfair that the National Union, which is now profiting by a large increase in its numbers, from the interest which has been aroused all over the Kingdom by the actions of the militants, should fail to acknowledge their indebtedness to the self-sacrificing women of the Social and Political Union, who are now, and have been all along, bearing all the hard blows, and doing all the hard work of the campaign.
>
> All the commentators agree that the Pilgrimage was a triumph of organisation in marked contrast to the wretched campaigns of the window-breaking and policeman-kicking section of the advocates of votes for women. The Kent section of non-militants – largely recruited from the Isle of Thanet – showed up well.[9]

A Margate lady sympathiser with the non-militant movement sent the *Thanet Times* a copy of Monday's *Daily News* containing an eloquent account of the demonstration.

> The Roman eagles never waved more triumphantly than the banners of the Women Pilgrims as they marched into Hyde Park on Saturday afternoon.
>
> It was a rare sight. For weeks and weeks, through long days and long summer nights, through rain and shine, the wonderful army of non-militant suffragists has been marching triumphantly on London town from all ends of the

country. It has been kind and cool; and if there has been little sunshine there has been less rain.

These women in the Park – hardly bronzed Englishwomen, tingling with high endeavour, moved by the best traditions of their race, with the tonic winds of the heath and hill still making music for them, and the memory of triumphant progress stirring them – these women were making a rare fuss over their kettle of fish. Why? Well, anyway, they could tell the tale! The trick of the tongue was theirs: they were nice and healthy and fresh and brown and earnest.

Nineteen platforms were ranged in a huge circle, with the Reformers' Tree as centre, and from these seventy-eight speakers held forth at various elevations of eloquence for a full hour, from five o'clock to six. Almost without exception the speakers were given a quiet hearing, and any attempt at roughness or hooliganism was speedily settled not by the police or "stewards" but by the crowd itself, to whose intellectual side this forceful demonstration made an appeal that was not to be denied.

Perhaps after this triumph of constitutional methods, even the militant of the Pankhurst-Kenney type will see the wisdom of mending their manners.[10]

The biological argument again

The editors of *Votes for Women* advised their readers to consult the current number of *Science Progress*. In which Dr W S Pembrey, biologist and lecturer in physiology, had expressed his views on the proper place of women.

> "The old-fashioned view of women's place in nature is, he declares, the one supported by biological knowledge. The slur cast upon our Victorian mothers has not been properly resented. It is true that they did not glory in competing in mental and physical contests with men, but they could and did bear large and healthy families.
>
> "The so-called higher education of women" he asserts, "is not a good idea for either women, man or the State. Education at a University for three or four years makes a considerable demand upon the bodily, mental and pecuniary resources of the women, and there is little doubt that these would be more useful to all concerned if they were devoted to, or reserved for, marriage."
>
> We leave it to our readers to decide which they prefer – Dr Pembrey's ideal of woman as a mere breeding machine, or the Suffragist's ideal of woman as a rational human being, with an individuality and personality which she is bound to develop every whit as much as a man is bound to develop his.[11]

A short section of Dr Pembrey's article "Woman's Sphere" was reprinted in the *Thanet Times*.

> The old-fashioned view of woman's place in nature is the one supported by biological knowledge. Woman's sphere was the home and family, for there she found ample opportunities for the exercise of her special gifts of patience, kindness and love of offspring.
>
> Her influence in the State was indirectly as great as that of man, for apart from the control she exercised upon man, she held in her hands the training of her sons and daughters in those early years during which character is most easily moulded.

Women in Kent

The responsibility of a family prevented her from becoming too much interested in herself or in intellectual problems. As a young woman she looked upon marriage as the aim of life, and as an experienced matron, with every wish for the happiness of her daughters, she kept the same ideal before them.

The term "old maid" was one of reproach; a childless marriage was a calamity, a reflection one or other or both partners.[12]

Women selling *Votes for Women*

The following poem written by two paper sellers appeared in *Votes for Women* in early August 1913.

One morning, at the break of day
We sallied forth, and chalk in hand,
We painted white the town of P____
We painted brown the sand
Not very awful were the words
Our passing left behind –
"Buy VOTES, a penny" was the bomb,
The policemen came to find

One said to us, in accents fierce
"Just tell me if you can
Of what is women made" Said we
"Of substance like the man",
"Of substance like the man" quoth he
(For 'twas a he of course)
"Of a spare rib, I think you mean"
And argued himself hoarse

But we, undaunted, waited till
His wrath began to sink.
He waved away our paper-
Kept his penny for a drink
"Buy VOTES" said one, "I'd rather see
Such women thrashed!" and slow
I turned my head and looked at him-
"Of course, not you, you know".

That afternoon we sallied forth
Armed with six dozen VOTES -
But we missed some priceless comments,
For we hadn't time for notes.
Some few looked scorn they could not vent
With nose in air.
Some few, with pitying smile,
Said "We don't think you're doing right!"
And all the while it is for these we fight

July-December 1913

> But almost all were friends, and kind,
> And very many keen,
> So in two hours, our papers sold,
> We left that happy scene
> Of hopeful work and glad endeavour
> Knowing our labours would find their thanks
> In those who would come to swell the ranks,
> And the Cause would go on for ever.

Women police constables

This article, re-printed from *Modern Life*, appeared in August 1913. It was yet another dig at the suffragettes following Mr Justice Philimore's suggestion that a woman police constable should be appointed in each petty sessional division

> We already have women warders in the gaols and women searchers and attendants at the police stations and elsewhere, and there is no sound reason why the principle should not be applied more publicly, in such places as the railway termini and in certain much frequented West End thoroughfares.
>
> At any rate, we do not see anything "revolutionary" in the proposal, for of course, women police would be detailed only for special duties and could never be expected to undertake the general work of the force, where steady nerves and brute strength are required. Thus, we could not anticipate any such comedy as would be provided by sending a posse of policewomen to cope with a gang of militant suffragettes on the rampage.
>
> Perhaps this is just as well for the suffragettes, as they could not expect from their own sex one tithe of the good humour and kindly forbearance under great provocation which has marked the police rencontres with the hysterical rioters. Rather would there be tearing of hair and scratching of faces, from which the militants would emerge second-best.[13]

This was an interesting suggestion but there is plenty of evidence that the women protestors were in fact treated quite roughly by policemen especially in London.

The Margate visitors' latest craze

> To be really smart at Margate this year (says a writer in *The Daily Chronicle*) you must first lose a brooch or bracelet, and then beg, borrow or steal a piece of chalk.
>
> It is rather difficult to see the connection, but a walk along the promenade, especially at the Cliftonville end off the town, soon solves the mystery.
>
> In the middle of a broad ashphalte (sic!) walk I saw a charming young lady, in a pink woollen jacket – it would be rather daring to face the Margate crowd this year without such a jacket, in one or other of the popular bright colours – on her knees busily writing on the ground. I stopped to see what her mission in life could be, and then I saw the words rapidly grow under her busy fingers as she wrote in large chalk letters:-
>
> **LOST**
>
> A gold chain bracelet with locket. Reward offered. Apply – (there followed the address of a well-known boarding house).
>
> Afterwards as I strolled along the promenade, I came upon many of these notices. Brooches, bracelets, purses, watches, bags, umbrellas – every article

Women in Kent

that a woman might drop unnoticed on the promenade, or leave on a deck chair, was advertised in this fashion.

But the notices are by no means confined to advertisements of lost property. All sorts of little romances are helped forward in this manner. Today I found several chalk messages of this nature:-

Meet me tonight at the bandstand – J M

One wonders what happy little seaside romance lies behind that message – what struggles and devices to elude the vigilance of stern parents, or to escape the chaff of friends. Margate is a rare old match-maker. Perhaps by this time J M is buying an engagement ring, or is to be the proud possessor of one.

Of course the ubiquitous suffragette is striving to turn the craze to advantage, and there is many a "Votes for Women" chalked on the ashphalte (sic!). There are also several half obliterated exhortions, such as, "Miss— Bring your suffragettes to convert Margate". Whether Miss— will take heed remains to be seen . . . for the official with whom I was speaking today told me that while the messages were permitted so long as they proved of service to visitors, there is no intention of allowing the promenade to be used for political propoganda (sic!).[14]

Militants attack on pillar boxes and telephone office

The suffragettes have apparently renewed their activities in the district, and their operations have on this occasion assumed a particularly inglorious aspect. It was discovered late on Monday evening that the public telephone call box which is situated opposite Holy Trinity Church had been entered, and the wire cut, thus rendering the call station totally useless. A quantity of suffragette literature had been left behind, and written on a card were the words "The place for Asquith and McKenna is Hell."

In addition to this utterly pointless and puerile attempt, it was discovered shortly before midnight on Monday that a quantity of black fluid had been poured into pillar boxes in Castle Hill Avenue and Shakespeare Terrace. The action of the chemical had resulted in the obliteration of a considerable number of addresses. In the case of a pillar box which is situated in Castle Hill Avenue, near the Gables, twenty-two letters were damaged. The bottle containing the fluid had been thrown into the box, and a quantity of suffragette literature had been thrust through the aperture. On the top of the box the words "Votes for women and down with the men" had been written.[15]

How a man sells papers

Votes for Women thanked all the members of their "newspaper corps" who had continued to sell the paper over the summer, whether while on holiday or by standing in for a regular seller while they were away.

Denis Howell wrote in *Votes for Women* describing his recent experiences as a male supporter of women's suffrage.

I had very peculiar feelings when I first commenced selling *VOTES FOR WOMEN* and the *Suffragette*. I felt, indeed, extremely conspicuous. But I

July-December 1913

soon began to feel all right, for I had not been standing long before two men came along and bought two copies. Then unpleasant and humorous remarks were addressed to me, some by people who were afraid I should hear them, and others by people who meant that I should hear them.

One woman would like to burn me. "There's a man Suffragette! I never saw one before!" This made me wonder in what way I was different from other men.

The papers are selling very well, being bought by friends and people who seem as if they really want to know more about the Woman's Movement. Here is a pleasant-looking minister coming along, and I feel sure he will have a copy, so I offer him *VOTES FOR WOMEN*.

"It's a great pity you have nothing better to do" he says, very sharply, and walks away.

A "nut" with his hair plastered down on his head, passes by with a grin on his face and then comes back and buys a copy of *VOTES*. Without even glancing at the cartoon, he tears it into four pieces, and flings it down at my feet. A feeling rises within me, but I let it die. The same fate happens to three copies of the *Suffragette*. All these petty remarks and incidents only make me more determined to come and sell every week.

Simply by standing in the street and holding out the papers I made nearly every person say "Votes for Women" and that is just what we want; only we want hundreds and thousands of people to shout "Votes for Women", not only with their voices, but with the heart and soul of them.

More men are wanted to show their sympathy in a practical way with the Women's Suffrage Movement. If you cannot be militant, then work for the cause by selling papers and by other constitutional methods. Let the people see there are some real manly men supporting the women in their fight for common justice – men to whom it makes not the slightest difference if they are laughed at. If people sneer at you look them straight in the face, and let them know you are serious![16]

This issue also includes a holiday advertisement for the Isle of Man – "The Land of Woman's Suffrage".!

In the first week of November Beatrice Chapman wrote to the local paper concerning the appeal to the militant suffragettes by the Bishop of Winchester asking them to abandon their militant methods for obtaining the vote. She also informed readers that

> ". . . in the official newspaper of the non-militants, *The Common Cause*, there appeared last week an article "Why we are not militant setting forth very clearly, but without bitterness, the reasons why the non-militants do not seek their just rights by methods of violence. Our refusal to take part in outrages is based, not as many militants think on cowardice, but on principle. Does it require no effort of courage for women unaccustomed to publicity of any sort to face unflinchingly "the fierce light that beats" not "on a Throne" but on a decorated waggonette, and drive slowly through the streets of Margate and Westgate advertising the great non-militant Pilgrimage? How could one tell

Women waiting for a race to begin at the newly opened swimming pool in Canterbury in about 1909

(considering the recent irritation of the people at the destruction of their letters) that the only danger one would encounter would be a ball flung violently into the waggonette by a well-dressed, but ignorant young man on the Oval.[17]

The Oval mentioned here was a sunken garden area on the cliff top in Cliftonville with a bandstand, popular with summer visitors. The bandstand was restored in 2005.

Women as councillors

Beatrice Chapman wrote another letter to the editor, this time about "Women as Councillors". She felt that it was the

> . . . paramount duty of women to serve on Municipal and County Councils" and that "women candidates have often much opposition to encounter in some towns owing to the genuine and well-founded fear of the prying eye of women, among those who have been in the habit of feathering their own nests at the public expense, and who want to be left in peace, and not worried with troublesome enquiries and suggestions, though this of course does not apply to the towns of Margate and Ramsgate. [She concludes that] . . .Confronted by such difficulties, and hampered by political disabilities how can you expect women to come forth in huge numbers and fight an almost hopeless battle? On the other hand educated men who have possessed the vote for so long, and should, we would think, have served a good apprenticeship in knowledge of its usefulness, are frequently too lazy and indifferent to use it.[18]

July–December 1913

THE SPREAD OF TANGO.
Arrest of a Militant Suffragette.

In this Punch cartoon of 26th November 1913 the bag of a very pretty young suffragette gets entangled with an attractive young policeman while he is trying to arrest her.

> **Punch cartoon**
> **5th November 1913**
> Two ladies facing each other. The caption reads "The fifth of November. Coming to our bonfire? Ra-ther. Whose house are you burning?"

H Alex Griffin of Canterbury Road, Westbrook responded to our intrepid correspondent sympathetically as follows:

> ... at the present moment when municipal affairs are being brought more prominently before the public, the letter in your last issue, signed by Beatrice E Chapman, must be of great interest to thinkers. There is no doubt in a borough like Margate women should be represented on the Council by some of their own sex, as the greater portion of the rate-payers in a town of this description, are directly or indirectly, women.
>
> The old-fashioned fungus-covered prejudice, which has in the past prevented both man and women from thinking clearly and justly of the desirability of having women serving on public bodies, is gradually but surely being wiped away ...
>
> It is not only apathy, or, as your correspondent suggests, the shackles of political serfdom, which prevents the right ladies from coming forward, but also the insincere way in which local politics are generally conducted.[19]

Beatrice Chapman's weekly letter on the same page continues on the same theme explaining that:

> Another reason I gave for more women not coming forward was that private residents, who have naturally more leisure at their disposal than business women or lodging-house keepers, if married, like myself, are not permitted by law to vote, or stand for election on County and Borough Councils, nor are their daughters allowed to if they reside with their parents, though they may be earning their own living as doctors, nurses, teachers, factory inspectors etc., etc., and be eminently suitable.

Women in Kent

When women do stand it is not always easy to get elected, for municipal elections are now run in close connection with the big political parties, and as women are denied the Parliamentary vote, and cannot stand as Members of Parliament, they are not popular as candidates with the party wire-pullers. Thus they have to stand as Independents, and their chances are so poor that few women have thought it worth while to stand.

Dr Ethel Smyth, suffragette and composer of the "March of the Women" anthem used on marches, had written to the Archbishop of Canterbury. He wrote that "though he did his best to understand what is going on, he utterly failed to comprehend how women of intelligence, cultivation and in some cases, apparently, of religious feeling, could adopt the cause of the intercessionists".[20]

In a letter to the editor from Beatrice Chapman about women's work, she claims that

> Some men there are that think that women have driven them from the labour market, and that the presence of women there is a danger and a menace to men. Do they suppose that women go into the labour market of their own free choice, or for amusement, or for any other reason than that the wage of the husband is not sufficient to keep up the decent conveniences of the household?

Then there are the girl clerks and typists pouring into London each day. Do they go for fun, or to snatch away the work from men? They go because they must work to support themselves. Women's work, too, which was formerly done in the home, is more or less machined now, and done in factories. If they undersell men, it is not their fault but their misfortune; it is because, being voteless, employers are at liberty to offer them a wage that is not a living one, and which they dare not offer to enfranchised men. Ninety percent of the sweated labour in this country is done by women, and of all the employers of sweated labour the Government, which professes to have the cause of the poor at heart, is the worst! It is not so long ago since men suffered from the same injustice and nursed the same grievances. What has altered their condition and raised their wages but the extension of the Franchise? Thinking-women wish to have a hand in the making of the laws, which shall ensure to women a decent living wage.[21]

STOCKINETTE BATHING DRESSES and Regulation SWIMMING COSTUMES
Prices from 1/11½ up.

Thanet Times
10th May 1913

July–December 1913

[1] TT 4th July 1913
[2] TT 11th July 1913
[3] KGCP 12th July 1913
[4] KGCP 12th July 1913
[5] FH 19th July 1913
[6] FH 26th July 1913
[7] TT 25th July 1913
[8] FH 26th July 1913
[9] FH 26th July 1913
[10] TT 1st August 1913
[11] VW 1st August 1913
[12] TT 22nd August 1913
[13] TT 8th August 1913
[14] TT 17th August 1913
[15] FH 6th September 1913
[16] VW 19th September 1913
[17] IOTG 1st November 1913
[18] IOTG 8th November 1913
[19] IOTG 15th November 1913
[20] KGCP 18th November 1913
[21] IOTG 6th December 1913

Chapter Eleven

January–August 1914

> Oh we don't want to lose you, but we think you ought to go,
> For your King and your Country both need you so.
> We shall want you and miss you, but with all our might and main
> We shall cheer you, thank you, kiss you,
> When you come back again.
>
> (This rousing jingoistic song became one of the most popular recruiting songs of the First World War.)

1914 was a difficult year for the suffrage campaign. Yet again the women were let down in Parliament and continued to fight for the vote against the background of the Kaiser's sabre rattling and threats.

As Ramsgate women read this advertisement in the *Thanet Times* of 2nd January 1914 they could have had no idea about how the year would end! Please note that there are no men in this picture! There were 16,332 women registered as living in Ramsgate in 1914.

The suffrage movement

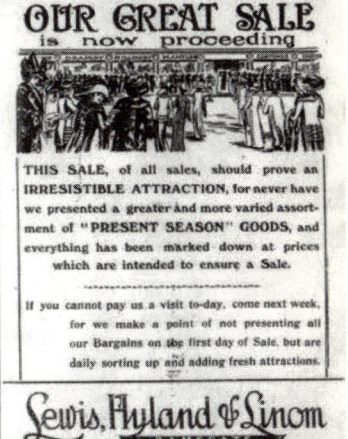

The NUWSS, in reviewing the position at the end of 1913 says, "Throughout the year the battleground was transferred from the country to the House of Commons, and here women were led to believe that there was to be finally a free vote on the merits of the question when the amendments to the Franchise Bill were discussed . . .

It is not necessary to recapitulate the fiasco of that week in January. None of the pledges given by Mr Asquith in 1911 was fulfilled. The refusal of the National Union (NUWSS) to accept in any sense as an equivalent the promises of the Prime Minister to give facilities for the discredited expedient of a private member's bill might have been a foregone conclusion. It resolved to concentrate on the demand for a Government measure, and to develop the policy of the union by increasing pressure on the Government in the constituencies, directing attack on the seats of Anti-Suffragist Ministers, and further strengthening the position of the only party in the House of Commons which had made women's suffrage an integral part of its policy.

If the year which has gone has been the most strenuous which Suffragists have ever had to face, that of 1914 promises no abatement of their energies whatsoever. Increased work to the constituencies, the collection of larger funds, further educational campaigns to demonstrate the forces existing behind the demand for the vote – these are the tasks which claim and will

St Georges Terrace, Canterbury

undoubtedly procure still greater resources of wealth and organisation. Early in February the union will hold its annual council, to decide its political programme, to be followed immediately by a great mass demonstration in the Albert Hall on February 14th to voice the united and constitutional demand from all classes throughout the country for a Government measure for Women's Suffrage.[1]

Social evening

Margate NUWSS Suffrage Society held a Social Evening in January at St John's Hall, Margate.

> Some orchestral music was delightfully rendered by Mrs Ainsley, piano, Miss Eva Harvey, violin and Mr Thornton Bobby, 'cello, varied by songs from Mrs Southey and Miss Cuthbert, and a recitation by Mrs Harris, assistant organiser for Kent.
>
> Miss Griffiths-Jones, National Union Organiser for Kent, briefly explained the objects of the Society, which was non-party and non-militant.[2]

Mrs Thornton Bobby was a supporter of women's suffrage. The family owned a piano shop in Cliftonville and still own two shops in Thanet to this day.

The servant problem

> The servant problem continues. Among my own immediate circle of friends (writes "Florence") I have not heard of any great difficulty in procuring domestics and retaining them, but evidently the trouble exists as so much is continually written on the subject.
>
> It is asserted that before a satisfactory settlement of the subject can be arrived at several radical alterations must be made in domestic service. It appears that some girls have objected because they are not put upon the same status as shop assistants and typists, and also because they are called by their Christian names.

January-August 1914

In many instances they are perhaps justified in making these complaints. After all, why should a girl, directly she enters a house, be called by her Christian name by people who are entire strangers, although it is surely more usual to use the surname, but without the desired "Miss" it is true.

Household work properly performed is as much a profession as typewriting, and if it is recognised as such, more girls may be willing to enter domestic service, more especially if they are given one or two hours daily in which their time is entirely their own.

It is the fact that girls working in offices and shops have so many hours which they can call their own that rouses the envy of domestic servants. If this reform were instituted it would make domestic service infinitely more attractive for, apart from what so many consider the one drawback, it provides a comfortable and healthy life for any girl. But if employers are to concede these points in favour of their household employees, the latter will be expected, in return, to make themselves entirely proficient in their work.[3]

A joint meeting of the NUWSS and the CLWS or Church League for Woman Suffrage was held in the Foresters' Hall in Canterbury on 27th March. Muriel Matters and the Revd Claud Hinscliff would speak at this meeting. The letter advertising this meeting ends with the observation that "the period of inactivity of the members of the Canterbury branch of the League for Opposing Woman Suffrage has coincided with a period of increased activity on the part of their opponents".[4]

In March 1914 Mary "Slasher" Richardson entered the National Gallery and slashed Velasquez' painting "The Rokeby Venus" with a meat cleaver. She claimed to have tried to destroy the picture of the most beautiful woman in mythological history in protest at the government's destruction of Miss Sylvia Pankhurst, who she claimed was "the most beautiful character in modern history."

The press and the militants

A male correspondent who describes himself as "an advocate of votes for sane women" makes the point that a recent correspondent to the paper wrote:

> At the beginning of our struggle the entire Press maintained a conspiracy of silence on the subject of women's demand for freedom, and so it was that, being denied the ordinary channels for bringing their need to the notice of the country, a comparatively small number of women took to burning houses and destroying letters to arrest the attention of the public, which method, if viewed solely from the point of view of attracting public attention, was, we are bound to confess, eminently successful! The Press was eager enough to publish the "outrages", for this meant increased circulation of their papers, but they still continued to ignore the large body of constitutional Suffragists. However, since the Suffrage pilgrimage of 1913 most of the papers have opened their columns to fair discussion of this important question of the day, notorious exceptions being those papers which are financed and controlled by a certain section of rich men, who desire to see women kept in subjection.[5]

In the same paper was the following article:

> **A scare**
>
> In these days when incendiarism forms a part of the active propaganda of the militant females who falsely pretend that they want votes for all women, it is

not, perhaps, surprising that the Pankhurst brigade were credited on Saturday with having caused a fire at Kingsgate Castle.

As it turned out the fire had nothing to do with the militant suffragists – the ablest and most resourceful of them were, happily, in prison, refusing to be fed, and imagining themselves heroines – poor understudies of Joan of Arc, and people of that sort.

One of the coastguardmen who helped put out the fire told the reporter "what he would have done with any militant suffragist whom he chanced to catch on the premises. But what he said is fit only for masculine ears."

The speakers at the joint meeting of the NUWSS and CLWS in Canterbury on May 27th were interrupted by a group of anti-suffragists "who literally bombarded the speakers with some obviously carefully thought out questions, which were, withal, skilfully answered".[6]

Women in public life

Women already possess the same opportunities as men as candidates for election to Parish Councils, District Councils, Metropolitan Borough Councils and Boards of Guardians. For any of these bodies a woman may stand if she has reached the age of 21, and has lived for twelve months in the electoral area.

Women have made good use of these opportunities, and there are today (says a correspondent in *The Daily Telegraph*) 1,536 women Poor Law Guardians in England and Wales. There are still, however, 194 Boards of Guardians which have no woman member, and every effort should be made throughout the country to get at least one woman elected to each of these Boards.

When we come to the County Councils and Borough Councils, we find that, through the absence of the residence qualification, the position of women is very different.

The only women who are eligible for these bodies are women whose names are on the burgesses' roll, i.e. widows or single women who possess the occupier's qualification. In London a married woman can stand for the County Council if she is an occupier or householder in her own name, but throughout the rest of the country married women are unable to obtain an electoral qualification in any way.

The result of this restriction is that it is very difficult to secure an adequate number of women candidates for Town and County Councils, as only those women who possess the municipal vote are eligible to stand. At present there are seven women on County Councils, and between twenty and thirty on Borough Councils. There is no doubt that if the residence qualification were provided for these Councils, the number of women candidates would immediately increase very rapidly.

It is only since 1907 that women have been eligible at all, and since that time a private member's bill has been introduced again and again to provide the residence qualification, but through the indifference of Parliament, the bill has been dropped every time.

It was very good news to hear from Mr Herbert Samuel, the President of the Local Government Board, a few weeks ago that he intended to introduce a bill on behalf of the Government. When this bill becomes law it will remove a

January-August 1914

barrier which at present keeps many women from giving their much-needed services to the work of local government.

Women are needed on Town and County Councils for many reasons. These Councils have to administer the Education Acts, and this involves in these days not merely the instruction of the children, but their medical inspection and treatment, feeding and so forth.

It is true that there are today 677 women doing very good work as co-opted members of Education Committees, but co-option to a committee can never be the same as election to the Council itself. The Education Committee is not the Education Authority – what is done by the committee must be ratified by the Council. Besides the work of education, a Municipal Council also has to do with housing, public health, and sanitation, and by the establishment of such institutions as milk depots and health visitors it can do much to stem the tide of infant mortality.

Many Acts of Parliament which might be very useful are only permissive in their character, and if the Municipal Councils do not adopt them they may have become a dead letter. It is important to have as much variety as possible among councillors, so as to ensure the fullest use being made of legislation.

We naturally think first of these parts of a councillor's work which appeal most strongly to women as women – to their mothering and housekeeping instincts, but, as a matter of fact, there are no municipal questions which do not interest women as human beings as much as they do men, even though they may be matters of finance, rating or general policy.[7]

Votes for women

This was an article written by a "miserable mere man" about an NUWSS meeting in Cecil Square in Margate on Thursday 14th May.

The meeting was called for 3 o'clock. It being a women's meeting it did not begin until 3.15. Perhaps the principal speaker's hat was not on straight. Or there may have been a difficulty about the blouses which button up behind. Bright and happy young women went around trying to sell copies of a weird publication admirably called *The Common Cause*. Our representative, in a moment of unusual profligancy [sic], bought one, and wants his money back. Eighteen adult ladies and one child swarmed round a waggon, on which two orators, Miss Geraldine Cooke and Miss Murray, were insecurely seated. Two ladies tried to paste up a contents bill. The wind was against them, and after many futile attempts the ragged remains of the poster hung disconsolately at the rear of a very ordinary cart.

Before the great meeting really began – it is horrid how indifferent the laundresses of Margate are to this great appeal – fair emissaries of the NUWSS buttonholed the few men who chanced to be passing through the Square, and one with bright blue eyes and golden hair sold the reporter his copy of *The Common Cause*.

When Miss Cooke told the audience (now numbering nearly 30) that the women of England were unanimous in their demands for votes, the nasty 30 people remained cold and unresponsive.

In the evening of Tuesday the ladies of the NUWSS (Margate branch) (Non-militant, non-political) had another meeting; and the tale was told in the same style with the same sort of cold, unresponsive audience. The fact is that the militancy has frozen the movement, and the work of the NUWSS is a labour in vain.

He then quotes from an NUWSS leaflet:

> When people hear of women's suffrage for the first time, they are often inclined to say at once that only men should have the vote, because women's sphere is in the home. If by this they mean that in most cases, when a man marries, he has to go on working outside his home in order to support his family, while, when a woman marries, she generally has to stay at home in order to look after it and all that is in it, I think we all agree about this. But suffragists think that it is just because women do think so much of their homes, and care so much about them, that they ought to have votes. For, if you come to think of it, there are lots of homes that can't be made clean and decent and orderly, however hard the women who live in them try to make them so. There are houses so badly built, and so inconvenient, that they make work faster than the women can keep up with it. There are houses with several storeys, and no water except on the ground floor: and there are houses with no water at all. There are many houses with none of the decencies of life, and there are some that are built "back to back" so that no fresh air ever gets through them. Then the surroundings are sometimes so foul that bad smells come through the windows and up the drains, and all sorts of dirt gets tracked in from outside. And, worst of all, there are houses with only two or three rooms, and ten or eleven people living in them. How can a woman keep her home nice and her children clean and good, when she lives in a house like these? Everyone knows it is impossible.

He ends his report with the comment "Of course with propaganda on these lines, women will presently get votes for a few of their sex."[8]

On 21st May 1914 a Big deputation marched to Buckingham Palace in an attempt to deliver a petition to King George V. Fifty-seven women were arrested including Mrs Pankhurst.

When war broke out in August 1914 many women were opposed to it. On 1st August 1914 Millicent Garrett Fawcett had written in the *Manchester Guardian* that "in this terrible hour, when the fate of Europe depends on decisions which women have no power to shape" the women of the IWSA or International Woman Suffrage Alliance called "upon the Governments and Powers of our several countries to avert the threatened unparalleled disaster", but by the time their anti-war meeting was held at the Kingsway Hall in London on 4th August it was too late.

January–August 1914

The authors' grandparents, William and Elizabeth Willatts, in 1914

---

[1] TT 23rd January 1914
[2] TT 30th January 1914
[3] TT 20th February 1914
[4] KGCP 28th February 1914
[5] TT 20th March 1914
[6] KGCP April 4th 1914
[7] TT 1st May 1914
[8] TT 22nd May 1914

Chapter Twelve

Women of Kent on the front line

Let us show ourselves worthy of citizenship, whether our claim to it be recognised or not. (Millicent Garrett Fawcett)[1]

August to December 1914

The Britain declared war on Germany on 4th August 1914. Two days later Millicent Garrett Fawcett announced that the NUWSS was suspending all political activity until the conflict was resolved. The NUWSS transformed itself into a Women's Active Service Corps to "assist in sustaining the vital energies of the nation".[2]

Following the announcement by the government that it would release suffragette prisoners due to the outbreak of war Mrs Pankhurst announced on 13th August 1914 that there would be a "temporary suspension of activities" by the WSPU. *The Suffragette* newspaper was renamed *Britannia* and dedicated "For King, for country, for freedom". Sylvia Pankhurst and her supporters began to set up a chain of relief centres for the poor women and children in the East End of London.

Mrs Ada Teetgen, press secretary of the Margate NUWSS wrote to the editor of the *Thanet Times* to inform him that the local branch had "suspended its ordinary political work for the time being and is prepared to use the entire organisation of the Union for the help of those who will be the sufferers from the economic and industrial dislocation caused by the war," and that Mrs Southey, the President of the Margate Branch of the Society, had informed the Mayor of Margate that "her committee is prepared to place their services at the disposal of any Committee which he may call together for such a purpose".[3] The Press Secretary for the National League for Opposing Woman Suffrage wrote to the Canterbury newspaper in similar vein adding that "the provision of garments for use in hospitals is also of urgent necessity" and that patterns approved by the Red Cross Society could be obtained from the Jackanapes Society in London.[4]

On 30th August 1914, encouraged by a number of writers, including the leading anti-suffragists Mrs Humphrey Ward and Baroness Orczy, retired Admiral Charles Fitzgerald founded the Order of the White Feather in Folkestone. Young women set off to present white feathers to educated young men who were loafing about instead of setting an example to working men by enlisting in the King's Army. Soon this somewhat unsavoury practice was used as a means of applying pressure to all able-bodied men to answer Lord Kitchener's call "Your country needs you" and join up.

These women became unpopular when they began presenting feathers to men invalided from the trenches, or otherwise unqualified for military duty, such as state employees or those working in key state industries. Many people felt that Reginald McKenna, the Home Secretary, should arrest these women. The government's response was to produce a badge bearing the legend "King and

Country", thus marking out its wearer as someone effectively excluded from overt moral pressure to enlist.

Baroness Emma Orczy, author of *The Scarlet Pimpernel*, went on to found the Active Service League which urged women to sign the following pledge:

> At this hour of England's grave peril and desperate need I do hereby pledge myself most solemnly in the name of my King and Country to persuade every man I know to offer his services to the country, and I also pledge myself never to be seen in public with any man who, being in every way fit and free for service, has refused to respond to his country's call.

Prominent members of the WSPU, such as Emmeline Pankhurst, Christabel Pankhurst and Annie Kenney, began to tour the country speaking at meetings to recruit young men into the army. Later in 1915 Christabel used the pages of *Britannia* to demand military conscription. Her supporters handed the white feather to every young man they encountered wearing civilian dress and bobbed up at Hyde Park meetings with placards saying "Intern them all".[5] Later in the war Thanet households started displaying War Discs in their windows. Each disc displayed represented one man who had volunteered to fight.

Within weeks of the outbreak of war *Gazette* readers were being advised to "Buy British" and "Support your own country". Mr Sackett, the Margate grocer asked "Why eat German sausage?" when he had just secured one thousand 6lb tins of Fray Bentos Corned Beef from Argentina.[6]

People in East Kent started to panic buy and it was suggested in the *Thanet Times* that it was the Margate shopkeepers themselves who had started the panic as they had put up their prices quite unreasonably. Well-to-do people, who could afford the higher prices, were accused of buying up supplies to feed their households for weeks to come, which made the staple goods more scarce and therefore more expensive for everyone else. As many summer visitors were self-catering this meant they could no longer pay these inflated prices, and by the end of the week many grocers were wishing they had given the food away.

Some room bookings were cancelled but most visitors finished their holidays and returned to London as planned. The *Thanet Times* was anxious to convey to its readers that it was " business as usual" and that there was no need to panic: "All along the route from Herne Bay to Margate harvest operations are in progress just as usual. Golfers are still discovering where the bunkers are on the local course, the motor trips are as well patronised as ever." They hoped that visitors would not "believe everything they are told or hear".

There was even a friendly dig at Ramsgate where "everyone will walk in the middle of the street. They are still doing so, and motor-cars can only crawl through the town at a snail's pace. Shops are busy, there are ample supplies, and the amusements are going on in just the ordinary way."[7]

Getting organized

Local groups of women in Thanet began to organize collection of funds and goods for distribution to the needy, at home or on the "front line". The Red Cross and the Soldiers' and Sailors' Families Association collected clothing and bedding. Some ladies helped with equipping and preparing schools and large houses as emergency

Women of Kent on the front line

hospitals. Thanet MP Norman Craig offered his home, Fairfield House in Broadstairs, as a hospital for wounded soldiers. In September 1914 the Working Guild of the Red Cross Society held a grand concert in the Queen's Highcliffe Hotel in Margate to raise funds for material for "the making up of garments for our soldiers and sailors". Every seat was booked within twenty-four hours of advertising.

> Miss Phyllis Dare [*right*] sang the recruiting song "Your King and Country want You". Copies of the song were sold in the room, the entire profits of the sale being devoted to the Queen Mary's Work for Women Fund. The song, written and composed by Paul Reubens, who accompanied Miss Dare on this occasion, has a fine, bold, martial air, which seems to carry the feet along with it.[8]

The disrupted summer season came to a close and seaside towns in Kent settled down to the first winter of the war. By autumn the fund-raising and gift-collecting was in full swing. Weekly lists of donors appeared in the papers:

> Ladies' Working Guild – 43 slings, four bandages, six water bottle covers, seven day shirts, three night shirts, eleven pairs bedsocks, bedjacket, two pillows and dressing-gown
> Miss Smithson 2 Surrey Road – five blankets, counterpane and a box of bandages
> Anonymous – a parcel of magazines
> Mrs Lee 22 Hatfield Road – three pillows, blanket, counterpane and two crutches
> Miss Lamberton 7 Cliff Terrace – bundle of books, spitting cup, spray, tin of groats(!), pestle and mortar
> Mr Povey 19 Addiscombe Road – camp bedstead, wool overlay, oil lamp, bed pan[9]

Women in Kent
To Men of Kent and Kentish Men

Your brothers in arms o'er the water
Are bearing the brunt of the show
Will you stand aside, nothing daring?
Men of Kent, Kentish Men, answer "No".
Our enemy's forces are mighty
Don't forget that this struggle is keen.
Some day you'll describe to your children
The greatest of wars ever seen.
Just picture the "Garden of England"
Devastated, wrecked, shattered and torn
Every village, town, borough and hamlet
Pillaged, ruined, burnt and left forlorn

Such fate, as the people of Belgium
Are so nobly enduring today,
May be ours if we don't end this struggle
"Might" must not be "Right" let us say
Accounts of lust, pillage and murder
Stir all Englishmen's souls to bed rock
Remember our Wellington's motto
Up and at 'em my lads, now, why not?
The honour of mothers and sisters
Wife, children, and all you hold dear
Demands that you give them protection
Such call surely manhood must hear

Your hearths and your homes all bear witness
To the peace that has so long been ours
Will you suffer them now to be trampled
'Neath armed foot? Not for hell and its powers
'Tis certain our overseas kinsmen
Will back us to win in this fight.

They are giving their men and their money
To crush the accursed "Might's Right".
Our cause is a true and a just one
Our honour we dare not deny
We are bound by the firm bonds of friendship
With France our fierce foe to defy.

No father or mother will wish you
To hold back or relinquish your part
In defence of our Homeland of England
Though piercing them through to the heart.
Men of Kent, these lines are appealing
Your country, your freedom to save
You, most of you, sing "Rule Britannia"
Are you willing yourself as a slave?
Count the cost ere pledging your honour
Comfort, ease (May God spare it) your life
It means sacrifice for your country
Your parents your children, your wife.

A Man of Kent[10]

Women of Kent on the front line

I suspect that this deliberate listing of donors and their addresses was to cause embarrassment to those who were not so listed, or might have encouraged more donors to remain anonymous. These lists were published throughout the war. The variety of items is amazing although there is no clue to the age or condition of the items donated!

Beatrice Chapman continued to write to the newspapers on topics of interest to women . In October 1914 she protested against the re-introduction of the Criminal Diseases Acts in Plymouth. "To hurl such an insult at womanhood just now of all times, when the women of England are suffering and sacrificing so much and so nobly for love of their country, is unthinkable." She was angry that in a Christian country under sanction of law a group of women were to be "instruments of the legalized lust of men" and concluded that "these evils can only be overcome by moral, and never by legislative, means".[11]

In November 1914 William Booth Reeve, the Mayor of Margate throughout the war, appealed to "my fellow townsmen for funds to supply our English wounded soldiers now being taken care of by our Red Cross with a view to supplying them with cigarettes, pipes, tobacco, and other little luxuries which they all so richly deserve."[12] Women were put to work making and filling sandbags for the trenches. Sadly as I was writing this book, nearly a hundred years later, a very similar letter appeared in our local Thanet newspaper appealing for funds for the Army Benevolent Fund, which is supporting soldiers and families of those serving or killed in action in Iraq and Afghanistan.[13]

The first contingent of 150 wounded British soldiers from the fighting in France arrived at Margate on a Sunday afternoon in November 1914. A large crowd gathered at the station gates to cheer the men as they were driven off in motor cars to local hospitals. There were six VAD or Voluntary Aid Detachment hospitals in Thanet, one of which was Quex Park House in Birchington. Belgian wounded were also being cared for in Margate. There was a large hospital for Canadian soldiers at the Granville Hotel on Ramsgate's Eastcliff.

By December it was becoming fairly obvious that "our boys" would not be home by Christmas. In December a widow highlighted the plight of many widows with children "who, because the late husband and father happened to be a civilian, cannot obtain help and have not a farthing but what they earn". She asks why these women, many of whom are educated, cannot be employed as auxiliary postmen and sorters. She felt it was unfair that when there was so little work about for women, soldiers' wives were going out to work and receiving an allowance while other women got no financial help.[14]

Although reconnaissance flights were made over the North Sea towards England by German airships, the first actual attacks were made by aeroplanes. In December 1914 a couple of bombs were dropped in the sea off Dover, and three days later, on 24th December, the first German projectile hit English soil. A small bomb fell near the Castle at Dover and broke some glass. On the following day a seaplane dropped a few bombs at Sheerness without causing any damage. The ground and aerial defences both responded but it was British aeroplanes that were affected most by the anti-aircraft fire from the ground.

Women in Kent

1915

In 1915 Beatrice Chapman tried her hand at poetry. This example is very typical of the sentimental verses published early in the war.

In Time of War

A sunny face though an aching heart
A strong resolve when it's right to part
Kind, friendly deeds where scant thanks are given
When evil reigns firm faith in heaven[15]

A rather more personal story is told in this moving poem written in the same month:

The Widow

I am stitching alone by the fire
Alone in my sorrow and pain:
I have given my man for his country,
My all; for England's gain

He never again will guard me
I must live alone with my love
And trust that he is still near me
And pray to the One above.

His child will come to remind me
Of the happy days gone by
I must put my grief behind me
And stifle my lonely cry

One hope alone I cling to
That the land for which he died
Will remember a hero's widow
And the child of a hero's bride.[16]

This poem has particular poignancy for me as my own grandmother was left in this position in October 1918 when my grandfather died of his injuries in Northern France. My father was born the following March so never knew his father.

The graphic realism of the poetry of Wilfred Owen and Siegfried Sassoon was yet to come. Many women wrote poetry during the war as well of course, and a good selection can be found in the *Scars upon my Heart* anthology published by Virago Press in 1981. Interestingly women poets write about different aspects of the war than men. There are plenty of "front line" poems about dying soldiers in military hospitals, written I suspect to express the writer's grief during the long hours of night duty, but also poems about life in a VAD kitchen, women doing men's work at home, knitting socks for a soldier who may not live to wear them, being left alone with unfulfilled dreams when a fiancé is killed in action, and a lament for the demobilized soldiers who on returning to Blighty after the war discover that the "the land fit for heroes" they have been promised does not quite live up to expectations.

Women of Kent on the front line

Not all suffragists supported the war. Sylvia Pankhurst, Emmeline Pethick-Lawrence and many others were opposed to the war, and worked tirelessly to bring an end to the hostilities, playing an active role in organizations such as the Women's Peace Party.

In the House of Commons in March 1915, the Prime Minister Mr Asquith dismissed women pacifists, saying: "This is not the time to talk of peace." Such talk was "like the twittering of a sparrow amidst the stress and tumult of a tempest". He then repeated his Guildhall declaration of November 1914 saying these were the only terms upon which Britain should sheathe the sword.

By the spring of 1915 there were real fears about the coming summer season during which most of Thanet's residents earned a living. A large number of women earned their income taking in summer boarders. A large number of itinerant entertainers and tradespeople also relied on the seaside summer trade. There were of course many other visitors to Thanet in 1915 including Belgian refugees and, over the year, more and more wounded soldiers, or those needing to convalesce. The refugees were identified by their black, orange and red ribbons. In June a plea was made for funds to pay for city children to be able to enjoy a seaside holiday.

According to a letter to the editor of the *Isle of Thanet Gazette* it cost "10s per fortnight per child, or 12s 6d for a disabled child". The writer regarded this work "even in war time, not as a luxury, but as a vital necessity. Many of the children now being sent away have fathers enlisted in His Majesty's Forces, and one can easily picture in such homes the special boon conferred by this friendly interest and care."[17]

Early in April 1915 the *Isle of Thanet Gazette* reprinted an article that had appeared in the previous Wednesday's *Daily Telegraph*:

> To certain people it may be a surprise to learn that, the war notwithstanding, and even despite the withdrawal of the railway companies of cheap holiday tickets, the popular watering-places in the Isle of Thanet . . . are preparing for Eastertide just as usual . . . and these seaside communities are regarding the future quite hopefully . . . The war to be sure, has cast a shadow over most of our health resorts . . . But our famous watering-places have no notion of "going under".[18]

The following week the same paper reported that: "The town was not as crowded as usual" but "Margate had a busier Easter than the most sanguine at one time had hoped for. The hotels in Cliftonville were full . . . the municipal entertainments and other attractions were well patronized."[19]

All sorts of fund-raising ideas were tried. In May 1915 the Red Cross Society held a "Pound Day". Donors were not asked for money but for pounds of staple household food items such as butter, currants, sugar, jam, tea etc..

A letter to the editor in June expressed the fears of many:

> Sir, It is no use disguising the fact that Margate has been, and will be, severely hit by the prevailing condition of affairs.
>
> It is quite likely that the bulk of the people here, who depend upon visitors, may be able to get through the summer somehow or other, but the prospect for next winter is, for most of them, appalling. It would seem that now is the

Women in Kent

time for the best brains of the town to meet and endeavour to formulate some scheme for dealing with the subject. What is wanted are long and broad views and level-headed statesmanship. Yours Truly "H"[20]

Work in seaside towns had always been seasonal and by the summer of 1915 some families in Thanet were struggling, but, as this article points out, not only the working classes were experiencing straightened circumstances.

> The conditions that prevail in Broadstairs are peculiar, and differ somewhat from those in most other towns, as there are no factories or special trades in the district and the majority of the inhabitants earn their living by letting lodgings, and secure their harvest in the summer season, when crowds of visitors bring the means to pay rent and taxes, with something over. Last year, owing to the war, there was no season, and many persons found themselves seriously straitened. In times of stress it is usually the very poor, or the working-classes who feel the pinch: under present conditions . . . this is not the case: there is plenty of well-paid work for those who will work, while the liberal separating allowances granted by the Government to the families of soldiers and sailors have made many humble homes much more comfortable than they were before the war. The want of money has been felt in a different class which never appeals for help unless the need is very great.[21]

On 17th May 1915 German Zeppelin airships started a "strategic bombing" campaign against England. Twenty incendiary bombs were dropped over Ramsgate and the Bull and George Hotel in the High Street received a direct hit. For the next three-and-a-half years East Kent was bombarded from the air and sea. The women who had stayed at home suddenly found themselves on the "front line" and it was a terrifying experience.

The Bull and George Hotel in Ramsgate

Women of Kent on the front line

Advertisements for household products such as Sunlight Soap increasingly showed "Tommies" or regular soldiers and sailors. A Sunlight ad in October 1915 contained a quotation from the Labour MP Will Crooks which suggested that men at the front were kept going by idealized visions of the little woman at home by the fireside.

This image of "Keep the Home Fires burning", another popular song from the First World War, was used throughout the second half of 1915 to advertise gas fires! Soldiers deliberately sent cheerful postcards and letters from France, censored by their superiors, in most cases cleverly disguising the truth. My own grandfather's letters asked for some "pommade" to get rid of the "Germans" in his shirt. Soldiers in the trenches were plagued with lice as they could not wash or change their clothes for months on end.

Despite gloomy forecasts and silly stories told by the sensational press of "yards of barbed wire on the Sands and Promenades" and Zeppelin raids, visitors were not deterred from visiting Margate over the August Bank Holiday weekend, although "the shadow of the war" hung over the town.

> "This August Bank Holiday, of course, there were no steamboats. There was no restaurant open, no dainty teas, no luncheons, no incidental intervals for refreshments during which confidences might be exchanged between busy men from town snatching a brief holiday; the kiosks were untenanted; even the inevitable angler at the northern end of the jetty baited his hooks with reluctant worms in a sad sort of way, as if he didn't really want to do it. [There was however] . . . still entertainment to be found in the Jetty Pavilion, where the stalwart "Corinthians" entertained the visitors with an excellent and varied programme.[22]

In September 1915 a film of *Lord Kitchener's Recent Visit to the Trenches* was the main attraction at local picture houses. In October the offering was *War is Hell – Thrilling Episode of the Great European War*. Fewer entertainers came down from London but there were an increasing number of military band concerts for fund-raising. Recruiting rallies also continued.

On 13th September 1915 the first daylight raid by an aeroplane took place. Bombs were dropped over Cliftonville and two women were killed. One lady was buried in the Jewish cemetery at Ramsgate and her tombstone bore the words "Killed by a German bomb".

Nurse Edith Cavell was shot On 12th October 1915 by the Germans in Brussels for helping English soldiers to escape from her military hospital.

This reproduction of an Arthur English postcard is from the Imperial War Museum's collection.

Women in Kent

In November there was some fear expressed that "The Dilemma of Darkened Windows" would reduce Christmas trade, so local firms were encouraged to advertise their wares in the local newspapers. Readers were reminded that "Photographs for the front must be posted early". Another plea on 6th November 1915 was "Who will adopt a wounded soldier?" Women were making or buying Christmas puddings for putting in parcels sent either to prisoners of war or to the trenches. A "Little League of Helpers" was set up in Broadstairs to pack up the parcels.

The toy trade had been particularly badly hit by the war as there were no longer imports of German toys, but at Bobby's in Margate in December 1915 they were offering "wonderful wooden toys made by disabled soldiers and sailors in the Lord Roberts' Memorial Workshop" and were coping with "a large demand for model forts, boxes of soldiers, model cannon and anti-aircraft guns, men o' war etc." For girls there were special dolls "dressed in the latest fashion in Messrs Bobby & Co's own workrooms".[23]

The first ten postwomen or letter carriers started work in Ramsgate in mid-December. Westgate already had one. Women were already working as ticket collectors and conductors in Thanet. Following the trend, women who worked in grocer's shops were called "grocerettes".

1916

In January 1916 Thanet was mourning the loss of many local men when HMS *Natal* was bombed in a harbour in Scotland on 30th December 1915. The local newspapers were full of articles about soldiers "mentioned in despatches" or obituaries for "a man who could always be depended on to do his bit".[24] The Hippodrome in Margate was holding regular Sunday afternoon services for soldiers during the winter. Those who contributed to the Mayoress' fund had sent 140 Christmas parcels to "our boys". The Mayor was finding it difficult to write his New Year's message. Despite "the terrible world-wide strife" he urged townsfolk not to forget those less fortunate than themselves at home, many of whom had made heavy sacrifices.[25]

Sir Henry Lucy, an eminent journalist, visited Miss Stancomb-Wills at her home on the East Cliff at Ramsgate at the end of January 1916. He wrote a regular "London Letter" which was read all over the country. While he was in Ramsgate there was a German bomber attack on Dover which could clearly be heard on the Ramsgate promenade at about midday on Sunday. The War Office, however, reported it as "Air Raids on the East Coast of Kent". Sir Henry thought this was hard on the Thanet seaside resorts as they were already struggling to attract visitors. "A state approaching destitution exists among the boarding-house keepers" and many hotels were half empty. He had stayed near the Granville which had now become a hospital. It felt strange to see "groups of wounded soldiers in their blue uniforms" where once there had been "highly-paying guests". He said that on sunny days "The Parade is crowded with members of the blue brigade, some with only one arm left, many walking on crutches, all cheerily drinking in renewed health and strength." Since the Granville was not big enough for all the patients, many were billeted with local boarding-house keepers.[26]

Women of Kent on the front line

On 9th February 1916 there was another daylight raid on Ramsgate but luckily most of the bombs dropped in open fields over the Montefiore Estate at the north-eastern end of the town so no-one was killed. A baby died in a raid on Cliftonville at the beginning of March but the worst tragedy was on Sunday 19th March when a group of children in Ramsgate were killed on their way to Sunday School.

In February 1916 one of the first marriages took place between a wounded Canadian soldier and his Ramsgate bride. Private Chiverall hopped proudly along on his right leg (having lost his left one) as his ward mates used their crutches to form a guard of honour for Sidney and his bride Elizabeth. This photograph taken, by Mr Siminson of Ramsgate, was one of the most poignant to appear in the local paper.[27]

Another Canadian Private who was a patient in Minster Hospital wrote the following tribute to his nurses.

Our Nurses

We sing of Jack and Tommy and the glorious deeds they've done
On every piece of land and sea wherever there's a Hun
Why not sing of our brave nurses – God bless them every one
Who have volunteered to tend the boys until the victory's won?

They too have left behind them loved ones the same as us
And gladly go where duty leads and never make a fuss
They have gone to France and Belgium, Serbia and the Dardanelles
And I believe if they had their way they'd follow the boys through ____!

A big convoy arrives at the hospital, some badly wounded, that's true
But nurse still smiles as she asks them all "Anything I can do for you?"
Then see her softly stealing in the solemn watches of the night
Like a guardian angel, to see that all is right.

Now and then you'll hear a groan from some poor soul in pain
Nurse will gently tend to him, then tuck him in again
No wonder the boys like a wound – and a month or so in ward
For they'll all tell you with a smile they've had a trip to Heaven

One of these glorious women was murdered by the Hun
Because she dared to stay and face a duty nobly done
Look out, you dirty square-heads, who think you're hidden from view
May God have mercy on your souls when Tommy gets after you!

So when speaking of Jack and Tommy let all of us bear in mind
That we must not forget our nurses, so generous and kind
Then let's all take our hats off to these heroines of ours
And do not wait until they're dead to offer them the flowers.[28]

In 1916 the Royal Engineers established a Stores and Personnel Depot at Richborough near Sandwich in Kent capable of handling 30,000 tons of supplies per week. Later the port was expanded to provide a cross-channel barge service.

The first Alexandra Rose Day had been held in 1912 to commemorate the fiftieth anniversary of Queen Alexandra's arrival among her British subjects. In Folkestone in June 1913 the ladies sold over 20,000 roses and collected almost £220 for the Royal Victoria Hospital in Folkestone. In September 1914 the first generally recognized flag-day was held, organized by Agnes Morrison in Glasgow. It was called Union Jack Day and money was collected in aid of the Soldiers' and Sailors' Families Association and the Territorial Force Association. The original flags were red, white and blue ribbon, stitched to matchsticks. By April 1915 £300,000 had been raised by various flag days. New regulations were brought in to monitor street collections. Collectors, who were usually women, had to be at least sixteen years old, and permits were granted to societies rather than individuals.

The 29th April 1916 was a fine Saturday for flagsellers. Some started as early as 6am and soon the St George's cross appeared in every buttonhole: "The man who can resist a flag when presented by a flag-seller does not dwell in the Isle of Thanet." The "cross" ladies were seen at every vantage point in the town. Ramsgate and Broadstairs between them raised about £140 that day – a lot of money in 1916.[29]

Zeppelins (often abbreviated to "Zepps") were still in use as well and there were further raids throughout the summer. Sir Douglas Haig was appealing to the nation on a Government poster to "Postpone your holidays" and "Support the men at the Front". The people of East Kent must have felt that they were doing more than their fair share.

By the summer of 1916 the local newspapers were full of obituaries of Thanet men missing or killed in action. Many of them had photographs of the casualties in their uniforms too. Families began to dread the sight of the telegram boy cycling up the road as it usually meant that someone had died.

In September 1916 most cinemas in East Kent were showing the official war picture *The Battle of the Somme* which was billed as the greatest film of all time and was 5,000 feet long![30]

Mrs Julia Ward from the Women's Freedom League came to speak to the Margate Pioneer Society in November 1916. Mrs Thornton Bobby presided at the meeting. Mrs Ward said "she was glad to meet with intelligent women whose minds were seriously engaged with things besides the immediate awful conditions of war, and who were concerned to prepare for the difficult time which lay beyond". Women's contribution to the war effort both in paid and voluntary work had proved that women deserved full citizenship and she should have a say in the management of that state that she had served and "with which her life was bound up, and which had power over the life and death of her sons". She added that now was the time to prepare the ground for their "sacred cause" as when so many women were doing men's work and "often doing it better" why should they not be given the vote? "After the war women must be ready to finish the fight begun ten years ago which had been temporarily relinquished in order to render aid in that other bloody fight that her brothers had brought on the world."[31]

1917

In February 1917 Margate and Broadstairs were shelled from a destroyer just off the Kent coast. In March ships were attacked in Ramsgate Harbour. The Royal Flying Corps began using Manston aerodrome in 1916 and it was attacked in April 1917. In February 1917 German submarines sank 230 ships bringing food and other supplies to Britain. Britain was, however, getting better at increasing

Women of Kent on the front line

food production and the wheat harvest of 1917 was the best in our history.

On 11th March, 1917, the Commander-in-Chief of the British Army, Sir Douglas Haig, wrote to the War Office accepting the principle that women could work in France, but his overriding concern was that women simply would not be able to do the physical labour of the men. He also did not want them to work in clothing storerooms as men had to change in these, and he felt a woman's presence there would be unacceptable.

The Women's Army Auxiliary Corps was organized into four units: cookery, mechanical, clerical and miscellaneous. To be accepted into the WAAC you had to provide two references and go before a selection board as well as have a medical. The WAAC had no officer ranks to it – just controllers and administrators. Pay in the Women's Army Auxiliary Corps was dependent on work done. Shorthand typists could get 45 shillings a week; 12 shillings six pence was deducted per week for food though uniforms and accommodation were free.

In April 1917 Mrs E R Dunn of Ramsgate read a paper on "Women – Their Work" to the Margate Pioneer Society. In the section on women's work for their country she felt that:

> . . . most people's opinion had been altered, and their outlook widened lately by the way in which women had been 'doing their bit' – they had even read of a lady private secretary to the Prime Minister! Women had been given appointments in the National Service Scheme, and three million were said to be available for further service.
>
> Leading men and the Press had insisted on the success of, need for, and readiness for women's extended employment as munition workers, carpenters, gardeners, engine and ship builders etc.. Huts in France, big guns and machine guns, ships engines etc., had been built almost entirely by women labour. It was the fashion for women to be tanned in a manner impossible to attain except by honest labour in the open. It was endurance and thorough employment of the brain , muscle and intelligence, and not by the exercise of the homekeeping arts, that women were helping the country to win the war.
>
> Necessity, a law unto itself, had swept away the barriers to their employment in certain trades considered to be unwomanly. Strength and ability had proved to be alike, whether in trousers or petticoats. But they had to remember that the sense of proportion must be preserved; and while grasping firmly the ideals of the new era of usefulness and opportunity, the fundamental principles of home-life must not be lost. It was still true that the hand that rocked the cradle maintained the Empire.[32]

Mrs Peel, a director of the Women's Service at the Ministry of Food came to Margate on 9th May 1917 to speak at a public meeting about the Food Control Campaign. On 25th April Lord Devonport had said in the House of Commons that "Food in this war was destined to be a supremely decisive factor. We must eat less."[33] Potatoes and flour were in short supply. Women in Broadstairs were invited to classes in war cookery, learning how to find substitutes for rare commodities and also how to use hay boxes for cooking. Houses started to

Women in Kent

display "In Honour bound" cards which were issued by the Food Control Campaign to show households where people were trying to limit what they ate. They also issued glass preserving jars for fruit and vegetables.

On 25th May 1917 bombs were dropped on the Canadian camp at Shorncliffe, just outside Folkestone, where there were 100 casualties. Then one bomb fell in a crowded street in Folkestone and killed 33 people, mostly women who were out shopping. On June 17th a Zeppelin again attacked Ramsgate Harbour and destroyed the Fish Market. The home of the anti-suffragist Miss Weigall was also damaged. In August two Gotha bombers were brought down over Thanet.

On 19th June 1917 the Women's Suffrage Clause was passed at the committee stage in the House of Commons by 385 votes to 55, a bigger majority than expected, and on 7th December the Representation of the People Bill was passed giving very limited franchise to women over 30 – the dyke had been breached.

In August 1917 the Central War Work Committee in London asked the women's employment committee in Broadstairs and St Peter's to provide 1,000 shirts a week.

In September 1917 a branch of the Girl Guides was started by Mrs Sandeman-Allen in St Peter's. The aim of the movement was to develop good citizenship among the girls and teach them a sense of patriotism, self-reliance and a sense of duty. Every age and class of girl was welcome to join.

During the autumn of 1917 raids by both Zeppelins and aeroplanes continued. At the end of October Ramsgate Gas Works received two direct hits.

In December 1917 500 women from Thanet went to work at Richborough Port sorting salvage from the battlefields.

Just before Christmas a German bomber (below) developed engine trouble and was forced to land in a field near Margate, where as can be seen opposite it was destroyed by the crew before they were taken prisoner.

Women of Kent on the front line
1918

War weariness had set in as more and more food restrictions were introduced. Panic buying led to shortages and so in January 1918, the Ministry of Food decided to introduce rationing. Sugar was the first item to be rationed, later followed by butchers' meat. The idea of rationing food was to guarantee supplies, not to reduce consumption.

Meat was especially scarce and in January 1918 "The Butchers of Margate" announced in the IOTG that they "have decided to close their shops from Saturday night until Thursday morning!" Meat cards were valid in butchers' shops or in exchange for a meat dish at a restaurant. In the IOTG of 23rd February 1918 some advice for "bewildered card-holders" appeared. There were also a number of recipes appearing recommending the use of meat substitutes. Butter and margarine were also scarce.

In the IOTG of 5th January 1918, a public appeal from the Mayor William Booth Reeve was published earnestly requesting that the "The people of Margate" respond to "His Gracious Majesty the King" and attend a place of worship on the following Sunday for "Earnest Supplication for Guidance and Strength" and a "Divine Blessing upon our Empire" in this "The gravest crisis ever known".

Advertisements offering air raid insurance began to appear in the local newspapers but in fact the last air-raid in East Kent took place in July 1918. The people of Thanet were asked to "Buy Bonds and Certificates to provide a Thanet aeroplane", or to collect "Waste Paper for Munitions". Advertisements started to appear such as "Young widow seeks situation as typist".

There were fewer shows in the theatres but the picture houses or cinemas were thriving, with the home-grown talent of Charlie Chaplin topping the bill many weeks of the year.

In March 1918 Thanet's Conservative Central Council decided that "to a limited extent, women electors should work in conjunction with the existing Associations"[34] and among the ladies who were nominated to serve on the Central Council were Miss (later Dame) Janet Stancomb-Wills and Mrs E R Dunn of Ramsgate (who were already Ramsgate Borough Councillors), and Mrs Hatfield and Mrs Fenner for Margate.

Norman Craig MP told the meeting that they

> ... wished to prepare for the future in the same way that preparations were being made for dealing with after-the-war problems, and had congregated so that the women, who had become possessed of the power to vote, might be prepared before they were called upon to use their power. Although the vote had only been granted to the women of the country under limited conditions, his view was that there would be more equality before long.

He went on to say that there would be an "immense upheaval" after the war and that "the duty of the women voters in the interests of the country was to get ready". "Organise, and be ready when the time for action comes," exhorted Mr Craig.

Women in Kent

In July 1918 every household in Dover received instructions about how to prepare their families for an evacuation of the town. The town was split into ten districts. The townsfolk were to meet at prescribed assembly points and await orders. Arrangements were made to supply water and tinned meat to the evacuees en route as they walked first to Acrise, then to Brabourne and finally to Ham Street, where trains would then transport them to the West Country. Luckily the German Army began its retreat that summer so it was never necessary to execute these plans.

By November 1918 the guns fell silent and the people of East Kent had to adjust to peace time conditions once more. When the war finally came to an end it was difficult to believe it at first.

> The great war, after lasting for a period of four years, fourteen weeks and two days, was officially brought to a close, it is hoped, at eleven am on Monday last, the 11th of November. Rumours of the signing of the armistice, which was confidently expected, reached Margate early in the morning, and flags were flown on a few buildings. It was not, however, until eleven o'clock, after official confirmation of the news, that the flag was run up at the municipal buildings, and the blowing of the "All Clear" on the sirens, which have in the past given warning of the approach of enemy aeroplanes, announced to the inhabitants the termination of hostilities. It was received with demonstrations of delight, and in a comparatively short space of time the streets were festooned with flags, and houses were freely adorned with bunting. The streets were soon thronged with people waving flags, and there was on all sides evidence of the delight with which the news was received after the long period of dreary war.[35]

Later that day the Mayor addressed the townsfolk in Cecil Square and the children were given the rest of the day off school. After singing the national anthem the children paraded through the town. Cheers went up for "the King, for the gallant and noble boys over the water, for all the Allies, and for the women".[36]

[1] CC 7th August 1914
[2] *The Suffragette Movement*, Pankhurst E Sylvia, Longman, London, 1931 (P 593)
[3] TT 28th August 1914
[4] KGCP 29th August 1914
[5] *The Suffragette Movement*, Pankhurst E Sylvia, Longman, London, 1931 (P 594)
[6] IOTG 8th August 1914
[7] IOTG 15th August 1914
[8] IOTG 26th September 1914
[9] IOTG 10th October 1914
[10] KGCP 12th September 1914
[11] IOTG 17th October 1914
[12] IOTG 21st November 1914
[13] *Thanet Adscene* 14th December 2006
[14] IOTG 12th December 1914
[15] IOTG 9th January 1915
[16] *Woolwich Pioneer* 22nd January 1915
[17] IOTG 19th June 1915
[18] IOTG 3rd April 1915
[19] IOTG 10th April 1915
[20] TT 5th June 1915
[21] IOTG 21st August 1915
[22] IOTG 7th August 1915
[23] IOTG 11th December 1915
[24] TT 14th January 1916
[25] TT Jan 7th 1916
[26] TT February 4th 1916
[27] TT 25th February 1916
[28] TT 18th February 1916
[29] TT 5th May 1916
[30] TT 15th September 1916
[31] TT 3rd November 1916
[32] TT 6th April 1917
[33] TT 4th May 1917
[34] IOTG 9th March 1918
[35] IOTG 16th November 1918
[36] IOTG 16th November 1918

Chapter Thirteen

Women's right to serve

Doing One's Bit
Girls are up and doing
Working hard all day
Driving motor vans or carts
In quite an English way

Women sit by firesides
For Jack or Tom to knit
No matter what our sex is
We're here to do our bit.

*Two verses from a poem by Hilda M Slade,
published in the* Thanet Times, *18th February 1916*

In August 1914 Queen Mary sent the following message to the "Women of Great Britain"

> In the firm belief that the prevention of distress is better than its relief, and that employment is better than charity, I have inaugurated the Queen's "Work for Women Fund." Its object is to provide employment for as many as possible of the women of this country who have been thrown out of work by the war. I appeal to the women of Great Britain to help their less fortunate sisters through this fund. Mary R.

This was the picture (*right*) of Queen Mary enclosed in the Christmas card sent to the troops with tobacco and chocolate for Christmas 1914.

The wages offered to the women in the East End, where many women were employed in the clothing industry, were only ten shillings a week. Sylvia Pankhurst called them "Queen Mary's Sweat-Shops".

By 1915 suffragists had turned from demanding the vote to promoting anti-German propaganda. Placing their recruiting skills at the disposal of the authorities they began to recruit women workers for the Home Front and the munitions factories. The Board of Trade issued a circular in March appealing to women to register at Labour Exchanges for War Service. An article by Mrs Emmeline Pankhurst appeared in the *Daily Sketch* of 23rd March 1915 giving reasons why women should be mobilized. Not all suffragists supported the war. Sylvia Pankhurst continued to campaign in East London for votes for women. While other women

Women in Kent

demanded the right to serve, Sylvia and her Workers' Suffrage Federation held meetings continuously demanding equal pay for women and safer working conditions.

The Women's Right-to-Serve demonstration was held in London on Saturday 17th July 1915 in pouring rain. Despite the atrocious weather, thousands of women from all classes, including contingents of munitions workers, or munitionettes, land girls and FANYs (First Aid Nursing Yeomanry) marched to demand the right to do munitions and other war work.

As the war progressed, of course, there were more and more opportunities for women to work and take over jobs previously done by men. As activist and journalist Ethel Alec-Tweedie put it: "Today every man is a soldier, and every women is a man . . .war has turned the world upside down; and the upshot of the topsy-turvydom is that the world has discovered women, and women have found themselves."[1]

By 1915 many women had a college or university education – many had trained as teachers and some as doctors and nurses, but other professions such as law, accountancy, and architecture, were now opening up to women. For girls who reached school certificate standard there were plenty of clerical, secretarial and shop assistant jobs. Women soon learned to operate typewriters and telephones, and also learned to drive, which opened up new job opportunities as chauffeurs and delivery van drivers.

By 1916 over 3,000,000 men had joined the army. In February 1916, all single men and childless widowers aged 18 to 41 were compulsorily conscripted into the armed forces. The Government now had to recruit women to fill the gaps left by the men. Overnight women became bus and tram conductors, chimney sweeps, signalmen, journalists, bakers, and policewomen, who were sometimes known as copperettes. Women also worked on the land on farms and in forestry, and also in the distribution and delivery of the produce. In February 1916 an article in the *Thanet Times* reported that by then "from 12,000 to 14,000 women had gone to the land since the outbreak of war" and that two of the most successful farmhands were tailoresses from London who were now working in Sussex. Miss La Motte of the Board of Trade added that "as milkers and stockswomen girls beat the men hollow. A cow that has always been milked by a women is always better tempered and gives more milk." By 1917 a quarter of a million women were working on the land in the British Isles.

DRIVEN FROM HOME BY A WOMAN.

On this postcard from the First World War the expression on the soldier's face says it all!

Women's right to serve

Women had been training to look after British soldiers on the battlefield before the war. The FANYs had been established in 1907. Before going into the field they had to qualify in first aid, home nursing, horsemanship, veterinary work, signalling and camp cookery. The VADs or Voluntary Aid Detachments had similar duties. Trained members of the British Red Cross and the Order of St John's Ambulance formed detachments to work at home and abroad. The first women's VAD in Kent was set up in Ramsgate in 1910. They were all trained in First Aid but some also trained in nursing, cookery, hygiene and sanitation.

A group of women doctors, surgeons and nurses set up the Women's Hospital Corps. Many of them were militant suffragists like Dr Flora Murray and Dr Louisa Garrett Anderson, daughter of Dr Elizabeth Garrett Anderson, England's first woman doctor, and niece of Millicent Garrett Fawcett, who spoke at a suffrage meeting in Dover in 1909.

In the early months of the war, the War Office claimed that it did not need the services of women on the Western Front. Dr Elsie Inglis from Scotland was told "My good lady, go home and sit still." The Women's Hospital Corps, disgusted by their rejection, went to Paris to set up a well-equipped hospital unit, staffed entirely by women, for the French Red Cross. They later opened a hospital in Wimereux near Boulogne. Detachments of VADs and FANYs also went to work in Belgium and France for the Red Cross. They ran field hospitals, drove ambulances, and set up soup kitchens and troop canteens, often in extremely dangerous and difficult conditions. Vera Brittain, the author of *The Testament of Youth* served as a VAD nurse in France. Some women also risked their lives fetching wounded soldiers from the trenches on stretchers within yards of the firing line.

In 1915 Sir Alfred Keogh, head of the RAMC, said that these women "were worth their weight, not in gold, but in diamonds"[2] and invited Dr Flora Murray and Dr Louisa Garrett Anderson to take charge of a large military hospital in Central London. The hospital in Endell Street, just north of Covent Garden, had over 500 beds and was again staffed entirely by women. By the end of the war they had treated over 26,000 patients.

In the House of Commons on 14th August 1916 Asquith praised the women's contribution to the war effort: "It is true they cannot fight, in the gross material sense of going out with rifles and so forth, but they fill our munitions factories, they are doing work which the men who are fighting had to perform before . . , and they have aided, in the most effective way, in the prosecution of the war."

Later as the war casualties increased the women of Kent found themselves on the front line as more and more wounded were brought back to Kent ports from the battlefields across the Channel in Flanders. People living in the coastal towns such as Ramsgate could actually hear the guns firing in Northern France when the wind was in the right direction. They also started using the tunnels in the chalk cliffs as air-raid shelters. Volunteers were also needed to look after large numbers of refugees. Many large houses, schools and hotels were prepared for use as VAD hospitals. Quex Park at Birchington, the home of the explorer Powell-Cotton, was one of the hospitals set up in East Kent. The women volunteers also worked in convalescent homes, rest stations, and medical supply depots.

As enemy bombing raids increased, more women volunteers were needed to nurse the civilian casualties at home as well. Dame Janet Stancomb-Wills, whose home was on the East Cliff at Ramsgate, refused to move throughout the war, even though Ramsgate was bombed heavily on a number of occasions. Dame Janet, an heiress of the Wills tobacco fortune, was created a DBE in 1919 for her generosity in funding the fitting out of warships.

In June 1923 Dame Janet was unanimously selected as Mayor of Ramsgate for the municipal year 1923–1924. By then in her seventies, she was somewhat reluctant to accept the post but Mayor Larkin praised Dame Janet's bravery in remaining in the town during the First World War despite the fact that her house was especially exposed to danger from air raiders and bombardment from the sea. Also during the war when the finances of the town were suffering because of the number of empty residences there and she assisted the corporation with a substantial loan. She also provided comforts and essential items for those who sought refuge in the air raid shelters in the cliffs.

In 1922 the Reverend Hertslet, Vicar of St George's Church in Ramsgate, commented that he was sure Dame Janet would have had no hesitation in leading a squadron of Amazons on the East Cliff during the war, repelling any attempt at a German landing with her own hands had the need arisen. He praised her for having sentiment without sentimentality, liberality without impetuosity.

Ramsgate certainly "bore the brunt of the attacks" and "the population was kept in a high state of tension". The people of Thanet remained defiant and "despite the constant danger from raids the population only dropped by one half of its 1914 figures".[3]

The suffrage societies were involved in recruiting women for work in the munitions factories. As Mrs Pankhurst said in January 1915 "I'm not nursing soldiers. There are so many others to do that. It is no more to be expected that our organisers should now necessarily take to knitting and nursing than that Mr Asquith should set his Ministers to making Army boots or uniforms." At first the trade unionists objected to women in the factories, fearing lower pay for women would deprive the male breadwinners of their jobs but, by the end of 1916, one-third of the workers in munitions factories, such as Woolwich Arsenal, were women, who became known affectionately as Munitionettes.

Wealthier women also helped with war charities, and worked as weekend relief for the

A munitionette

Women's right to serve

women workers in the factories. They ran canteens, organized the collection and distribution of clothes and other goods donated by the public, and gave generous donations to the war effort.

By 1918 the Ministry of Munitions of War was offering to train women to make aeroplane parts. Their poster ended with the encouraging words "If YOU follow up any of these lines of work and become proficient, YOU are definitely assisting the men in the fighting line."

The Women's Royal Air Force was also set up in 1918 to recruit female mechanics, but they were also advertising for "clerks, waitresses, cooks and experienced motor cyclists."

By the end of the war Board of Trade figures show that over 7 million women were in paid employment, which included 900,000 munitions workers.

---

[1] *Women and Soldiers*, FRGS, London 1918

[2] Fawcett, Millicent Garrett, *The Women's Victory – And After: personal reminiscences, 1911-1918.* Sidgwick & Jackson, London 1920

[3] Siminson, A H, *Ramsgate during the Great War 1914–1918*

Conclusion

The First World War strongly influenced the development of women's rights in Britain. It opened up temporary employment opportunities for many women who replaced the millions of men sent to fight in Europe. The Representation of the People Act was passed by the House of Lords in January 1918 and became law on 6th February 1918. Women over 30 years old who were occupiers of property, or married to occupiers, were entitled to vote. This amendment to the franchise was in large part due to the respect gained by all the women who worked successfully during the war in occupations usually done by men.

The *New Age*, reviewing Wilma Meikle's new book, *Towards a Sane Feminism*, said that she had taken advantage of the suffragist truce to consider whether the pre-war policy of the suffragists had actually been successful. She felt that "Women began at the wrong end; they wanted the symbol before it signified anything" and that if the women had devoted half the time, money, energy and brains that they wasted in training themselves for the more responsible positions of commerce and industry, thereby raising the economic status of women, then political enfranchisement would have been a lot nearer than it was.[1]

Millicent Garrett Fawcett maintained that:

> . . . the war revolutionized the industrial position of women. It found them serfs and left them free. It not only opened to them opportunities of employment in a number of skilled trades, but, more importantly even than this, it revolutionized men's minds and their conception of the sort of work of which the ordinary everyday woman was capable. It opened men's eyes to the national waste involved in condemning women to forms of work needing only very mediocre intelligence.[2]

In the introduction to her book *Women and the Great War*, Joyce Marlow disagrees with other historians who felt that "the pre-1914 feminist ferment was a waste of time and energy". She felt that the activists "were the rim of a dormant volcano that erupted solely due to the exigencies of the first industrialized total war" and concludes that "had the minority not been preaching the gospel of equal rights" the majority of the women may not have willing or able to grasp the opportunities presented to them by the absence of men during the Great War.[3]

Sadly it was to be another ten years after the Armistice before all the women in England were able to vote.

---

[1] *New Age*, 7th December 1916

[2] Fawcett, Millicent Garrett, *The Women's Victory – And After: personal reminiscences, 1911–1918,* Sidgwick & Jackson, London, 1920.

[3] Marlow, Joyce, *The Virago Book of Women and the Great War*, Virago, London, 1998

Appendix

When women around the world got the vote

New Zealand	1893
Australia	1902 (up to 1908 in different states)
Finland	1906
Norway	1907 (higher taxpayers) then 1913
Denmark	1915
Soviet Union	1917
UK	1918 (over 30) then 1928
Germany	1918
Poland	1918
Netherlands	1919
USA	1920 (but since 1869 in Wyoming)
Ireland	1922
South Africa	1930 (whites)
Turkey	1934
France	1945
Italy	1945
Japan	1945
China	1949
India	1949
Switzerland	1971

Index

A

advertisements 27, 141
air-raid shelters 153, 154
air raids 137, 140, 141, 142, 143, 144, 146, 147, 154
Anderson, Dr Elizabeth Garrett 6, 7, 10, 90, 153
Anderson, Dr Louisa Garrett 55, 153
anti-suffrage movement 45–52, 73, 81, 113, 128
Anti-Suffrage Review 46
anti-war movement 129, 139, 151–152
Armistice 148
Asquith, Herbert 73, 74, 90, 91, 125, 139, 153
aviation 16–17
    in wartime 137, 144

B

Baillie-Guthrie, Lavendar 20
Balfour, Lady Frances 57–58
Balgarnie, Florence 41
Bannerman, Sir Henry Campbell 8
banners 53–54, 58, 71, 84–85, 114
bathing 17
Becker, Lydia 6
Beese, Amelie (Meli) 7
Beresford-Hope, Mr (anti-suffragist) 9
Billing, Evelyn 95
Billington-Grieg, Teresa 9, 56–57
Birchington 13
"Black Friday" 77
Bobby's 31, 35, 142
Bodichon, Barbara Leigh Smith 6, 45
Brailsford, Mrs 89
Brassey, Lady 81, 84, 113
Britain, Vera 153
Britannia 133, 134
Broadstairs 13, 104, 106–107, 140
Broom, Christine 2

Brunyate, Dr Annie 83
Burkett, Hilda 87
Burns, John, MP 50–51

C

Canterbury 18
casualties 141, 143, 146
Cat and Mouse Bill 95, 99–100
Cavell, Edith 141
Cecil, Lord Robert 99
chalking 20, 60, 88–89, 117–118
Chapman, Beatrice 96–97, 138
    letters by 105, 106, 112, 113, 119, 120, 121–122, 137
checks, fashion for 36
Church League for Woman Suffrage (CLWS) 127, 128
Churchill, Lady Randolph 46
Clarion Vans 53
Cliftonville 13, 15, 104, 120
Coates, Dora Meeson 2
Cobbe, Frances 45–46
Cobden, Jane 9
Cockburn, Dr Douglas 63
Colquhoun, Ethel 47–48
Common Cause, The 21, 38, 48, 61–62, 64, 86
    distribution of 73, 88, 112, 114, 129
    on fashion 33
Conciliation Bill 74, 77, 78, 87, 89, 90
Cons, Emma 7, 9, 10
conscription 152
copperettes 152
corsets 33
councils
    in support of women's suffrage 82, 87, 89
    women's representation on 9–10, 120–122, 128–129
Craig, Edith 19
Craig, Norman, MP 74, 91, 112, 135, 147

Crooks, Will, MP 90
Curie, Marie 7

D
Dare, Phylllis 135
Davies, Emily 6, 7
Davison, Emily Wilding 106, 112
Deal 18
demonstrations 8, 53, 73, 90, 126
    see also pilgrimages
Despard, Charlotte 9, 64, 96
divorce 88
donors 135, 137
Dover 18, 31–32, 148
Drummond, Flora 83
Drummond, Victoria 89

E
election lunacy 48–49
enfranchisement 103–104, 112
    see also suffrage movement
entertainment 19–20, 89
excursions 18

F
Fabian Society 90, 91
FANYs (First Aid Nursing Yeomanry) 152, 153
fashion 23–38
Fawcett, Henry, MP 6, 101
Fawcett, Millicent Garrett (Mrs Henry) 6, 7, 8, 46, 58, 101, 129, 133, 153
Fawcett, Millicent Garrett 157
"female pills" 50
First World War
    months preceding 125–130
    women's fashion during 31, 38
    women's role during 133–148, 151–155
flag days 143–144
Folkestone 18
Food Control Campaign 145–146
food supplies 145–146, 147
footwear 27
force-feeding 58, 99, 100
Fox, Charles James 5
Franklin, Hugh 100
Freece, Walter de 20

Freud, Sigmund 51
"Friend's cards" 112
Frith, William 13

G
Gallichan, Mrs Walter *see* Hartley, Catherine Gascoigne
Garnett, Lucy M 46
General Elections 48–49, 67
Girl Guides 146
Gladstone, William Ewart 5
Gliddon, Katie 1
Goldstein, Vida 83, 85, 89
Gore-Booth, Eva (Countess Markievicz) 8
"grand council" of women 52
Grey, Charles, MP 5
Grey, Sir Edward 95
Griffiths-Jones, Miss Lynette 99, 101, 105–106

H
Haig, Sir Douglas 144, 145
hair 26, 38
Hamilton, Cicely 50–51, 62–63, 89
Hardie, Kier, MP 8, 90, 99
harem skirts 29, 82
Hartley, Catherine Gascoigne 51–52
hats 26–27
Haverfield, Hon Evelyn 89
Heaton, Henniker, MP 73
Hensley, Sophia Almon 48
Hill, Octavia 7
Hippodrome Theatre, Margate 20, 142
HMS *Natal* 142
hobble skirts 34, 48, 82
Holmes, Mrs 60–61
hospitals 135, 137, 142, 153–154
Housman, Clemence 89
Housman, Laurence 89
hunger strikers 58 *see also* force-feeding
Hunt, Henry 5
hysteria 51
Hythe 100, 113

Index

I
imprisonment 8, 58, 87, 88, 95, 96, 97, 101, 103, 133
Isle of Thanet Debating Society 43

K
Kenney, Annie 8, 87, 134
Kensington Society 6
Kentish pilgrimage 113–115
Keogh, Sir Alfred 153
Knight, Elizabeth 88–89

L
land girls 152
Lewis, Hyland and Linom 31, 125
Lloyd George, David 73, 96
Lloyd, Marie 19, 20
London Society for Women's Suffrage 6
Lovett, William 6
Lowndes, Mary 2, 54
Luxemburg, Rosa 7
Lytton, Lady Constance 89

M
Macaulay, Florence 70–71, 83, 87, 103
Macdonald, Ramsay, MP 90
Macfarlane, Mrs D H 41–42
Manhood Suffrage Bill 89
Mansell-Moulin, Mr C 63, 77–78
Margate 13, 14–15, 31, 117–118
Margate Pioneer Society 41, 54, 56, 144, 145
Marlow, Joyce 157
marriage 50–51
Married Women's Property Act 1882 6
Mary, Queen 151
Matters, Muriel 54, 85, 111, 113
meetings
    indoor 104–106
    open-air 59–64, 68–70, 75, 87, 103–104, 112
Meikle, Wilma 157
Men's League for Opposing Women Suffrage 63
Men's Union in Favour of Women's Suffrage 82

militancy 8, 42–43, 53, 54, 67, 87, 89–90, 92, 97–99, 100–101, 104–105, 118, 119–120
    guerila 10–11, 91, 95, 96
    publicity for 105–106, 114, 127–128
    "spiritual" 101
Mill, John Stuart 6, 58
"Mud March", the 8
munitionettes 152, 154
Murray, Dr Flora 55, 81, 153

N
National League for Opposing Woman Suffrage 133
National Union of Women's Suffrage Societies (NUWSS) 7, 10, 11, 51, 111, 113–114, 127, 128
    election policy of 64, 81–82
    Kentish Federation 76, 82
    Margate branch 54, 102, 106, 126, 129–130, 133
    Ramsgate branch 67, 70, 81–82, 90, 99, 102
    suspension of activities 133
needlework 27
Nesbit, Edith 7, 34
"new woman", the 6–7
non-militant pilgrimage 95, 106–107, 111–112, 113–115
nurses 143

O
Ogston, Helen 63–64
Orczy, Baronness Emma 133, 134
Order of the White Feather 133–134
outrages 97, 103, 119
outragettes 101

P
Pankhurst, Christabel 8, 53, 72, 83, 87, 134
    visit to Kent 75–76
Pankhurst, Emmeline 7, 8, 10, 47–48, 67, 83, 87, 96, 99, 133, 134, 151, 154
    visit to Kent 68–70, 76–77
Pankhurst, Dr Richard Marsden 6

Pankhurst, Sylvia 127, 133, 139, 151
parades 53–54
Parliamentary Franchise (Women's Bill) 81, 87
Pegwell Bay 13, 18
Pember-Reeves, Amber 57
Pembrey, Dr W S 115–116
Peterloo Massacre 5–6
Pethick-Lawrence, Emmeline 8, 9, 38, 58, 75, 78, 82, 83, 87–88, 89, 92, 100
Pethick-Lawrence, Frederick 9, 87–88, 92
petitions 41, 47, 103
pilgrimages 95, 106–107, 111–112, 113–115
poetry 25, 46, 49, 55, 67, 91, 112, 116–117, 136, 138, 143, 151
Poiret, Paul 34
Primrose League 58, 74

Q

Qualification of Women Acts
    1907 9
    1918 88

R

Rackham, Mrs 102
railways 13–14, 83
Ramsgate 13–14, 18
    anti-suffrage movement in 46–47
    shops 31, 32
rationing 147
recruitment 20, 134, 135, 151 *see also* Order of the White Feather
Red Cross Society 134, 135, 137, 139, 153
Reeve, William Booth 137
Reform Bill 95–96
refugees 139
Representation of the People Act 1918 146, 157
Representation of the People (Women) Bill 104
Richardson, Mary "Slasher" 127
Richborough 143

rights, women's 7
Roche, Raymonde de la 7
Royal Victoria Pavilion, Ramsgate 72
Russell, Alys 61–62

S

Sandhurst, Lady Margaret 9
Schreiner, Olive 84
seaside, the
    fashions at 29–32
    and the Votes for Women campaign 29
    during the war 134, 135, 139–140, 141, 142
servants 126–127
shops 31–32, 142
Slack, Bamford, MP 7
Smyth, Dr Ethel 122
Snowden, Ethel 5, 56–58
Snowden, Philip, MP 90
Soldiers' and Sailors' Families Association 134, 144
soldiers, wounded 137, 142, 143
sportswear 34, 35
St John, Christopher 89
St John's Ambulance, Order of 153
Stainer, Hilda 95, 97, 113, 114
Stancombe-Wills, Dame Janet 10, 147, 154
Stevenson, Flora 6
Stopes, Marie 7
stripes, fashion for 32
submarines 144
suffrage, men's 5–6, 7
suffrage movement 7, 125–126 *see also* Votes for Women campaign
    dissension within 9, 81, 88, 90, 92, 97
    early days of 41–43
    male support for 118–119, 127
    suffrage processions 70–71, 81, 83–85, 89
suffrage, universal 112
suffrage, women's 5
    arguments against 45–46
    history of 5–11

Index

suffragette colours 37–38
Suffragette, The 92, 100, 103–104, 133
suffragettes *see also* Votes for Women campaign
    origins of term 53
    style of dress of 23, 33
Swanwick, Helena 55

T
tailor-made gowns 32
Taylor, Helen 6
Territorial Force Association 144
Terry, Ellen 19
Thanet
    history of 13–21
    Votes for Women campaign in 42–43
Theatre Royal, Margate 70, 72, 78, 87
Tilley, Vesta 19–20
Titanic 86, 91
tourism 13–16
trippers 15–16, 29
trousers 30–31
truces 67, 77–78

U
Unexpurgated Case against Women's Suffrage, The 51–52

V
VADS (Voluntary Aid Detachments) 153
Victoria, Queen 45
vitrifragists 91
Votes for Women 9, 10, 33, 37, 64, 69, 71, 87–88, 88, 91, 92, 98
    distribution of 116–117, 118–119
    on Emily Davison 112
    fashion jottings 24
Votes for Women campaign 58, 129–130
    history of
    meetings 54–55, 56–58
    post-war 144
    at the seaside 20–21
    in Thanet 42–43

W
waistcoats 37
war widows 137, 138
Ward, Florence 101
Ward, Julia 144
Ward, Mr Arnold, MP 48
Ward, Mrs Humphrey 46, 48, 52, 133
Webb, Beatrice 7
Weigall, Lady Rose 46, 47, 57
Wells, H G 8
Westgate 13
"wife-made men" 74–75
window-smashing campaign 87–88, 89–90, 91, 97, 101
Winslow, Dr Forbes 63
Winter Gardens, Margate 19
Wollstonecraft, Mary 5
Wolstenhome-Elmy, Mrs 8
Woman Suffrage Bill 73
women
    incapacity of 49–51, 115–116
    as police 117
    in public life 128–129, 147
    right to serve of 152
    status of 10, 112
    war work of 134–135, 137, 146, 152–155
    working 103–104, 122, 126–127, 142, 145, 152, 155
Women's Active Service Corps 133
Women's Army Auxiliary Corps (WAAC) 145
Women's Freedom League 9, 60, 64, 96, 111, 144
Women's Hospital Corps 153
Women's National Anti-Suffrage League 46–47, 52
Women's Peace Party 139
Women's Royal Air Force 155
Women's Social and Political Union (WSPU) 7, 11, 78
    colours of 37–38
    suspension of activities 133
    in Thanet 70, 71, 74, 75, 87

Women's Suffrage Journal 6
Woodcock, Patricia 89
Work for Women Fund 151
Wright, Katherine 34
Wright, Sir Almroth E 51

Z
Zangwil, Israel 100
Zeppelins 140, 144
Zetkin, Klara 7